Essex

The Genealogist's Library Guide

Volume 1
Genealogical Sources

by
Stuart A. Raymond

Published by
The Federation of Family History Societies (Publications) Ltd.,
2-4 Killer Street, Ramsbottom, Bury,
Lancashire BL0 9BZ, U.K.

Copies also obtainable from:
S.A. & M.J. Raymond, P.O. Box 35, Exeter, Devon EX1 3YZ, U.K.
E-mail: stuart@samjraymond.softnet.co.uk

ISBN: 1 86006 086 2

ISSN: 1033-2065

First published 1998

Printed and bound by the Alden Group, Oxford and Northampton

Contents

	Introduction	4
	Abbreviations	6
	Bibliographic Presentation	7
	Libraries and Record Offices	8
1.	The History of Essex	9
2.	Local Histories	12
3.	Bibliography and Archives	17
4.	Periodicals	19
5.	Occupational Information	21
6.	Parish Registers and other records of births, marriages and deaths	25
7.	Monumental Inscriptions	31
8.	Probate Records	40
9.	Trade Directories, Maps and Dialect	46
10.	Official Lists of Names	49
11.	Records of National and County Administration	52
12.	Records of Parochial and Borough Administration	54
13.	Ecclesiastical Records	58
14.	Estate Records	66
15.	Education	76
16.	Migration	78
	Author Index	80
	Family Name Index	84
	Place Name Index	86

Introduction

This guide to published sources of genealogical information is intended primarily for genealogists. It is, however, hoped that it will also prove useful to historians, librarians, archivists, research students, and anyone else interested in the history of Essex. It is intended to be used in conjunction with my *English genealogy: a bibliography*, and the other volumes in the *British genealogical library guides* series. A full list of these volumes appears on the back cover.

Many genealogists, when they begin their research, do not realise just how much information has been published, and is readily available in printed form. Not infrequently, they head straight for the archives, rather than checking printed sources first. In so doing, they waste much time, and also impose needless wear and tear on irreplaceable archives. However, when faced with the vast array of tomes possessed by major reference libraries, it is difficult to know where to begin without guidance. This bibliography is intended to point you in the right direction. My aim has been to list everything relating to Essex that has been published and is likely to be of use to genealogists. However, anyone who tries to compile a totally comprehensive bibliography of Essex is likely to fall short of his aim. The task is almost impossible, especially if the endeavour is made by one person. That does not, however, mean that the attempt should not be made. Usefulness, rather than comprehensiveness, has been my prime aim — and this book would not be useful to anyone if its publication were to be prevented by a vain attempt to ensure total comprehensiveness. I am well aware that there are likely to be omissions, especially in view of the fact that, given constraints of time and money, it has not been possible for me to visit all of the large number of libraries with substantial collections on Essex's history. Each of them may well possess works not held anywhere else. The identification of such works is not, however, a major aim of this bibliography. Rather, my purpose has been to enable you to identify works which are mostly readily available, and which can be borrowed via the inter-library loan network irrespective of whether you live in London or Melbourne. Most public libraries are able to tap into this network; your local library should be able to borrow most items I have listed, even if it has to go overseas to obtain them.

In general, I have not included works which are national in scope but which have local content. Many such works may be identified in *English genealogy: a bibliography,* to which reference is made at appropriate points below. The innumerable notes and queries to be found in family history society journals etc., are excluded, except where their content is of importance. Where I have included such notes, replies to them are cited in the form 'see also', with no reference to the names of respondents. I have also excluded extracts from newspapers, and histories which have not been published. Where possible, citations are accompanied by notes indicating the period covered, the locality/ies concerned, and other pertinent information. Most of the items listed here have been physically examined to ensure that they are relevant, and that correct bibliographical details are given. However, a few items have proved elusive, and yet worthy of mention; these are noted 'not seen', and I cannot guarantee the accuracy of the information provided in these entries.

Be warned: just because information has been published, it does not necessarily follow that it is accurate. I have not made any judgement on the accuracy of most works listed: that is up to you.

If you are an assiduous researcher, you may well come across items I have missed. If you do, please let me know, so that they can be included in the next edition.

The work of compiling this bibliography has depended heavily on the resources of the libraries I have used. These included the Local Studies Department of Essex County Library at Colchester, the Essex Record Office, Chelmsford Library, the Institute of Heraldic and Genealogical Studies, the British Library, the Society of Genealogists, Guildhall Library, the University of Exeter library and the Exeter Public Library. All these institutions deserve my thanks, as do Brian Christmas and Meryl Catty, who have both read and commented on early drafts of the book. Mark Gant typed the manuscript, and Bob Boyd saw the book through the press. I am grateful too to the officers of the Federation of Family History Societies, whose support is vital for the continuation of this series. My thanks also to my wife Marjorie, and to Paul and Mary, who have lived with this book for many months.

Stuart A. Raymond

Abbreviations

C.A.	*Cockney ancestor*
E.A.H.	*Essex archaeology and history*
E.A.M.	*East Anglian miscellany*
E.F.H.	*Essex family historian*
E.J.	*Essex journal*
E.P.R.M.	*Essex parish registers: marriages*
E.Rec	*Essex recusant*
E.Rev	*Essex review*
E.R.O.	*Essex Record Office*
E.S.F.H.	*Essex Society for Family History*
F.H.S.	*Family history society*
M.G.H.	*Miscellanea genealogica et heraldica*
N.S.	*New series*
P.P.R.S.	*Phillimores parish register series*
T.E.A.S.	*Transactions of the Essex Archaeological Society*

Bibliographic Presentation

Authors names are in SMALL CAPITALS. Book and journal titles are in *italics*. Articles appearing in journals, and material such as parish register transcripts, forming only part of books are in inverted commas and textface type. Volume numbers are in **bold** and the individual number of the journal may be shown in parentheses. These are normally followed by the place of publication (except where this is London, which is omitted), the name of the publisher and the date of publication. In the case of articles, further figures indicate page numbers.

Libraries and Record Offices

There are many libraries and record offices holidng substantial collections relating to Essex genealogy; they cannot all be listed here. Various directories of libraries and archives are listed in Raymond's *English genealogy: a bibliography,* and these should be consulted. The major institutions are:

Local Studies Department,
Essex Libraries,
Central Library,
Trinity Square,
Colchester, CO1 1JR

Essex Record Office,
County Hall,
Chelmsford,
Essex SM1 1LY

1. ESSEX HISTORY

The purpose of genealogy is to trace our ancestral descent, and to attempt to understand our ancestors' lives within the context of the society in which they lived. These aims cannot be achieved without some appreciation of the historical background. The genealogist ought to read the standard histories of the county/ies in which his forebears lived, and ought to be aware of the various ways in which the sources used to construct family trees may also be used to recreate the world of the past. For Essex, a vast range of historical literature is available, and only a very summary listing can be given here. For further information, consult the bibliographies listed in section 3 below. A number of modern general histories of Essex are available:

EDWARDS, A.C. *A history of Essex.* 6th ed. Phillimore & Co., 1994.

JARVIS, STAN. *Essex: a county history.* Newbury: Countryside Books, 1993.

NEALE, KENNETH, ed. *Essex heritage: essays presented to Sir William Addison as a tribute to his life and work for Essex history and literature.* Oxford: Leopards Head Press, 1992.

NEALE, KENNETH, ed. *An Essex tribute: essays presented to Frederick G. Emmison as a tribute to his life and work for Essex history and archives.* Leopards Head Press, 1987.

BATES, MARTIN. *East Anglia: Norfolk, Suffolk, Essex, Cambridgeshire.* Regional military histories. Reading: Osprey, 1974.

Older county histories are frequently of more immediate use to the genealogist than their modern sucessors, since they frequently incorporated extensive extracts from original sources such as parish registers, monumental inscriptions, *etc.,* they often included pedigrees. The list which follows is arranged chronologically, by date of completion:

NORDEN, JOHN. *Speculi Britanniæ pars: an historical and chronological description of the county of Essex ... 1594,* ed. Sir Henry Ellis. Camden Society old series **9.** 1840. Includes list of principal gentlemens' houses.

MORANT, PHILIP. *History and antiquities of the County of Essex.* 2 vols. T. Osborne, reprinted with an introduction by G.H. Martin. Ilkley: Scholar Press, 1978. Parochial survey, with many descents of manors, *etc.*

A new and complete history of Essex ... 7 vols. Chelmsford: Lionel Hassall, 1771. Parochial survey, including descents of manors, memorial inscriptions, *etc.*

HUGHSON, DAVID. *London: being an accurate history and description of the British metropolis and its neighbourhood to thirty miles extent, from an actual perambulation, vol. VI.* J. Stratford, 1809. Parochial survey; this volume covers parishes in Hertfordshire and Essex.

LYSONS, DANIEL. *The environs of London, being an historical account of the towns, villages and hamlets within twelve miles of the capital, interspersed with biographical anecdotes.* 2nd ed. 2 vols. T.Cadell & W.Davies, 1811. Contents: v.1, pt. 1. County of Surrey pt. 2., Counties of Kent, Essex and Herts. v.2. County of Middlesex.

WRIGHT, THOMAS. *The history and topography of Essex.* 2 vols. George Virtue, 1836. Parochial survey, largely based on Morant's work.

SUCKLING, ALFRED. *Memorials of the antiquities and architecture, family history and heraldry of the county of Essex.* John Weale, 1845. Includes notes on various parishes, prints of brasses, *etc.*

OGBORNE, E. *The history of Essex from the earliest period to the present time ...* Chelmsford: P.H. Kelham, et. al, 1814. Parochial survey; covers the hundreds of Becontree, Waltham and Ongar (part), and the Liberty of Havering.

FISHER, WILLIAM R. *The Forest of Essex: its history, laws, administration and ancient customs, and the wild deer which lived in it.* Butterworths, 1887. Includes list of verderers, foresters, regarders, and kings woodwards.

For parochial surveys covering areas smaller than the county, see under 'Rochford Hundred', 'Stifford', and 'Tendring Hundred' in section 2.

The most important parochial survey of Essex is, of course, the Victoria County History:

The Victoria history of the county of Essex. 9 vols & 2 supplements to date. Archibald Constable, et. al., 1903-94. Alternative titles: *A history of the county of Essex,* and *The Victoria history of the counties of England: Essex.* v.1. [Natural history; early man; Essex domesday], ed. H. Arthur Doubleday & William Page. v.2. [Ecclesiasical history; political history; maritime history; social and economic history; schools; sport], ed. William Page & J.Horace Round. v.3. Roman Essex, with index to volumes I-III, ed. W.R. Powell, v.4. Ongar Hundred, ed. W.R. Powell. v.5. [Metropolitan Essex since 1850; Waltham Hundred; Becontree Hundred (part)]. v.6. [Becontree Hundred (part)] ed. W.R. Powell. v.7. [The Liberty of Havering-atte-Bower; Chafford Hundred (part)], ed. W.R. Powell. v.8. [Chafford Hundred (part); Harlow Hundred], ed. W.R. Powell. v.9. The borough of Colchester, ed. Janet Cooper.

There are numerous works dealing with particular periods of Essex history. The list which follows is very selective, and is biased towards general works based on sources of interest to genealogists. For ease of reference, the listing is arranged by period.

Medieval, to 1500

RITCHIE, NORA. 'Labour conditions in Essex in the reign of Richard II', *in* CARUS-WILSON, E.M. ed. *Essays in economic history.* Edward Arnold, 1962, v.2, 91-111. Reprinted from *Economic history review* 4, 1934, 429-51.

POOS, L.R. 'Population turnover in medieval Essex: the evidence of some early fourteenth century tithing lists', in BONFIELD, LLOYD, SMITH, RICHARD, & WRIGHTSON, KEITH., eds. *The world we have gained: histories of population and social structure.* Oxford: Basil Blackwell, 1986, 1-22.

POOS, L.R. 'Rural population of Essex in the later middle ages', *Economic history review* **38,** 1985, 515-30.

WARD, JENNIFER C. *The Essex gentry and the county community in the fourteenth century.* Studies in Essex history **108.** 1991. Includes lists of Commisioners of Array, members of the Commission of the Peace, etc., late 14th c.

POOS, LAWRENCE R. *A rural society after the Black Death: Essex 1350-1525.* Cambridge studies in population economy and society in past times **18.** Cambridge: C.U.P., 1991.

LIDDELL, W.H., & WOOD, R.G. *Essex and the Great Revolt of 1381: lectures celebrating the six hundredth anniversary.* E.R.O. publications **84.** 1982. Includes gazetteer of places connected with the revolt, with some names.

ORRIDGE, B. BROGDEN. *Illustration of Jack Cade's Rebellion, from researches in the Guildhall, together with some newly found letters of Lord Bacon, etc.* John Camden Hotten, 1869. Includes folded pedigree of Cooke of Gidea Hall.

Early Modern, 1500-1700

DAVIS, JOHN. F. *Heresy and Reformation in the South East of England, 1520-1559.* Studies in history series **34.** Royal Historical Society, 1983. Study of Kent, Essex and London.

COLDEWEY, J.C. 'The last rise and final demise of Essex town drama', *Modern language quarterly* **36,** 1975, 239-60. 16th c.

EMMISON, F.G. *Tudor food and pastimes.* Ernest Benn, 1964. Based on the archives of Sir William Petre of Ingatestone Hall.

EDWARDS, A. C. *English history from Essex sources, 1550-1750.* E.R.O. publications **17.** Chelmsford: Essex County Council, 1952. 252 extracts from miscellaneous records.

OXLEY, JAMES E. *The Reformation in Essex to the death of Mary.* Manchester: Manchester University Press, 1965.

EMMISON, F.G. *Elizabethan life: disorder, mainly from Essex sessions and assize records.* E.R.O. publications **56.** 1970. Collection of essays based on court records.

EMMISON, F.G. *Elizabethan life: morals and the church courts, mainly from Essex Archidiaconal records.* E.R.O. publications 63. 1973. Collection of essays on various subjects, based on ecclesiastical records.

EMMISON, F. G. *Elizabethan life: home, work and land, from Essex wills and sessions and manorial records.* E.R.O. publications 69. 1976. Essays on various subjects.

MACFARLANE, A.D.J. 'Witchcraft in Tudor and Stuart Essex', in COCKBURN, J.S. ed. *Crime in England, 1550-1800* Methuen, 1977, 72-89.

EMMISON, FREDERICK. 'Tithes, perambulations and sabbath-breach in Elizabethan Essex,' in EMMISON, FREDERICK, & STEPHENS, ROY, ed. *Tribute to an antiquary: essays presented to Marc Fitch by some of his friends.* Leopards Head Press, 1976, 177-215. Based on the act books of the Archdeacons of Essex and Colchester.

SAMAHA, JOEL. *Law and order in historical perspective: the case of Elizathethan Essex.* New York: Academic Press, 1974.

HUNT, WILLIAM. *The puritan moment: the coming of revolution in an English county.* Cambridge, Mass.: Harvard University Press, 1983.

SHARPE, J.A. *Crime in seventeenth-century England: a county study.* Cambridge University Press, 1983. Based primarily on Essex Assize and Quarter Sessions records.

HOLMES, CLIVE. *The Eastern Association in the English civil war.* Cambridge: C.U.P., 1974.

DANN, GRACE, ROWLAND, SUZANNE, & WRIGHT, DAVID. 'Civil War and political strife', *Colchester historical studies* 1, [1978], 5-21. Includes various lists of names of the 1640's.

KINGSTON, ALFRED. *East Anglia and the Great Civil War: the rising of Cromwell's Ironsides in the associated counties of Cambridge, Huntingdon, Lincoln, Norfolk, Suffolk, Essex and Hertford.* Elliot Stock, 1902. Includes lists of the committee men.

LYNDON, BRIAN. 'Essex and the King's cause in 1648', *Historical journal* 29, 1986, 17-39.

LYNDON, B.P. 'The Parliament's army in Essex, 1648: a military community's association with county society during the second civil war' *Journal of the Society for Army Historical Research* 59, 1981, 140-60 & 229-42.

CLARKE, DAVID T.D. *The siege of Colchester 1648.* Colchester: Cultural Activities Committee, [1975]. Pamphlet.

WOODWARD, DAPHNE, COCKERILL, CHLOE. *The siege of Colchester, 1648: history and a bibliography.* 2nd ed. [Colchester]: Essex County Library, 1979.

Modern, 18-20th centuries

SMITH, J.R. *The speckled monster: smallpox in England, 1670-1970, with particular reference to Essex.* E.R.O. publication 95. 1987.

BARKER, ROSALIN, *The Plague in Essex: study materials from local sources.* E.R.O. publication 85. 1982. Portfolio of facsimiles of original documents.

BROWN, A.F.J. *Essex at work 1700-1815.* E.R.O. publications 49. 1969.

BROWN, A.F.J. *Prosperity and poverty: rural Essex, 1700-1815.* E.R.O. publication 134. 1996.

BOOKER, J. *Essex and the industrial revolution.* E.R.O. publication 66. 1974. General history.

BURLEY, K.H. 'An Essex clothier of the eighteenth century', *Economic history review* 2nd series 11, 1958-9, 289-301. Based on bills, commercial correspondence and account books of Thomas Griggs.

BROWN, A.F.J. *Meagre harvest: the Essex farm workers struggle against poverty 1750-1914.* E.R.O. Publications 106. 1990.

SHARPE, PAMELA. 'Bigamy among the labouring poor in Essex, 1754-1857', *Local historian* 24(3), 1994, 139-44.

DAVIDOFF, LEONORE, & HALL, CATHERINE. *Family fortunes: men and women of the English middle class, 1780-1850.* Hutchinson, 1987. Scholarly study based on Birmingham and Essex sources.

WOOD, R.G.E. *Essex and the French wars 1793-1815.* E.R.O. publications 70. SEAX series of teaching portfolios 9. 1977. Contains numerous examples of original sources.

SHARPE, PAMELA. 'The women's harvest: strawplaiting and representation of labouring women's employment c.1793-1885', *Rural history* **5**(2), 1994, 129-42.

CUTTLE, G. *The legacy of the rural guardians: a study of conditions in mid-Essex.* Cambridge: W. Heffer & Sons, 1934. General study.

BROWN, A.F.J. *Chartism in Essex and Suffolk.* E.R.O. publication **87.** 1982. Published jointly with Suffolk Record Office.

GRAY, ADRIAN. *Crime and Criminals in Victorian Essex.* Newbury: Countryside Books, 1988.

HARDY, DENNIS, & WARD, COLIN. *Arcadia for all: the legacy of a makeshift landscape.* Mansell, 1984. Study of life in shacks and shanties in the 20th c., mainly in Essex.

2. LOCAL HISTORIES.

There are innumerable histories of particular places in Essex; a full listing would occupy the whole of this book, and cannot be attempted here. The works identified below all have a particular value to genealogists; they either include substantial extracts from original sources or have a wider importance than the merely local. In the latter category, modern works on Earls Colne, Havering atte Bower, and Terling have made a major contribution to the study of English history in recent years, and should be read by everyone interested in Essex history.

Ashdon
GREEN, ANGELA. *Ashdon: the history of an Essex village.* Privately printed, 1989.

GIBSON, ROBERT. *Annals of Ashton: no ordinary village.* E.R.O. publication **99.** 1988.

Aveley
See Stifford

Ardleigh
SUKOLL, THOMAS. 'The household position of elderly women in poverty: evidence from two English communities in the late eighteenth and early nineteenth centuries', in HENDERSON, JOHN, & WALL, RICHARD, eds. *Poor women and children in the European past.* Routledge, 1994. Based on evidence from the records of Ardleigh and Braintree.

Barking
LOCKWOOD, HERBERT H. 'Frogley's manuscript history of Barking', *C.A.* **66,** 1995, 33-7. Brief note on an important work.

Blackmore
JARVIS, CLAIRE. 'The reconstitution of nineteenth century rural communities', *Local population studies* **51,** 1993, 46-53. Discusses a reconstitution of the parishes of Blackmore, Willingale Spain, and Willingale Doe.

Bradwell Juxta Mare
BROWN, HERBERT. *History of Bradwell-on-Sea, Essex.* Chelmsford: J.H. Clarke & Co., 1929. Includes biographical notes on clergy, manorial descents, etc.

Braintree
See Ardleigh

Brightlingsea
DICKIN, EDWARD PERCIVAL. *A history of Brightlingsea: a member of the Cinque Ports.* 2nd ed. Brightlingsea: D.H. James, 1939. Includes biographical notes on clergy, manorial descent and many names.

Chadwell St. Mary
See Stifford

Chelmsford
GRIEVE, HILDA. *The sleepers and the shadows: Chelmsford: a town, its people, and its past.* 2 vols. E.R.O. publication 100. 1988- . v. 1 The medieval and Tudor story. v. 2. From market town to chartered borough.

Bulphan
See Stifford

Coggeshall
BEAUMONT, GEO. FRED. *A history of Coggeshall in Essex, with an account of its church, abbey, manors, ancient houses etc., and biographical sketches of its most distinguished men and ancient families, including the family of Coggeshall, from 1149, to the reunion at Rhode Island, U.S.A. in 1884.* Marshall Brothers, 1890. Includes monumental inscriptions, descents, notes on clergy, list of 17th c. funeral sermons, *etc., etc.*

Colchester

General
MARTIN, GEOFFREY. *The story of Colchester from Roman times to the present day.* Colchester: Benham Newspapers, 1959. General history.
MORANT, PHILIP. *The history and antiquities of the most ancient town and borough of Colchester in the county of Essex ...* T. Osborne, 1768. Appendix includes deed abstracts, monumental incriptions, *etc.*
STRUTT, BENJAMIN. *The history and description of Colchester ...* 2 vols. Colchester: W. Keymer, 1803. Includes monumental inscriptions.

Medieval
BRITNELL, R.H. *Growth and decline in Colchester, 1300-1525.* Cambridge: Cambridge Universtity Press, 1986. Includes bibliography.

Early Modern
HIGGS, LAQUITA. 'Wills and religious mentality in Tudor Colchester', *E.A.H.* 22, 1991, 87-100.
DOOLITTLE, I.G. 'The plague in Colchester 1579-1666', *E.A.H.* 4, 1972, 134-45. Based on parish registers.
WARD, JENNIFER. 'Wealth and family in early sixteenth century Colchester', *E.A.H.* 21, 1990, 110-17. Mainly local wills.

18-20th centuries
D'CRUZE, SHANI. *Our time in God's hands: religion and the middling sort in eighteenth century Colchester.* Studies in Essex history 3. E.R.O. publications 109. 1991. Includes pedigrees of Morfee, Lince, Dikes, Smythies, *etc.*
DOOLITTLE, IAN G. 'Age at baptism: further evidence', *Local population studies* 24, 1980, 52-5. Based on the registers of St. Mary Magdalene, Colchester, 1721-1812.
BROWN, A:F.J. *Colchester 1815-1914.* E.R.O. Publications 74. 1980.
CANNADINE, DAVID. 'The transformation of civic ritual in modern Britain: the Colchester oyster feast', *Past and present* 94, 1982, 107-30. 19-20th c.

Corringham
See Stifford

Dagenham
O'LEARY, JOHN GERARD. *The book of Dagenham: a history.* 3rd ed. Dagenham: Borough of Dagenham, 1964. Includes manorial descents, lists of rectors, lords and stewards, etc.
SHAWCROSS, J.P. *A history of Dagenham in the County of Essex.* Skeffington and Son, 1904. Extensive; includes memorial inscriptions, notes on clergy, lists of churchwardens and parish clerks, extracts from parish registers, will abstracts, manorial descents, *etc., etc.*

Earls Colne

MACFARLANE, ALAN, ed. *Records of an English village: Earls Colne 1400-1750.* 3 vols. 113 fiche. Cambridge: Chadwyck-Healey, 1980. v.1. Church records. v.2. State records. v.3. Estate records. This extensive work is an attempt to transcribe all surviving documents relating to the history of Earls Colne, including the parish register 1558-1765, probate records, poor law records, tax lists, *etc., etc.* Important.

MACFARLANE, ALAN, *The origins of English individualism: the family, property and social transition.* Oxford: Blackwell, 1978. Partially based on the records of Earls Colne, but an invaluable read for all genealogists and historians.

SREENIVASAN, GOVIND. 'The land-family bond at Earls Colne (Essex) 1550-1650', *Past and present* **131**, 1991, 3-37. See also **146**, 1995, 151-87.

East Ham

FRY, KATHARINE. *History of the parishes of East and West Ham,* ed. G. Pagenstecher. Aug. Siegle, 1888. Extensive; includes manorial descents.

East Tilbury

See Stifford

Elmdon

ROBIN, JEAN. *Elmdon: continuity and change in a north-west Essex village, 1861-1964.* Cambridge: Cambridge University Press, 1980.

STRATHERN, MARILYN. *Kinship at the core: an anthropology of Elmdon, a village in north-west Essex in the nineteen-sixties.* Cambridge: C.U.P., 1981. Scholarly study, includes pedigrees of Gamgee, Greenhill, Hammond, Hayes, Hoy and Reeves families.

Fobbing

BINGLEY, RANDAL. *Fobbing: life and landscape: essays on an Essex parish.* Stanford le Hope: Lejins Publishing, 1987. Mentions many names — but unfortunately has no index.

See also Stifford

Gestingthorpe

PATCHETT, ALFRED. *Notes on the parish of Gestingthorpe, Essex,* ed. C. Deedes and C.T. Bromwich. F.G. Robinson & Co., 1905. Primarily manorial descents and biographical notes on clergy.

Grays Thurrock

See Stifford

Halstead

HOLMAN, WILLIAM. *Holman's Halstead, being historical notes ...,* ed. T.G. Gibbons. 2nd ed. Halstead: W.H. Root, [18--?] Includes many extracts from original sources.

Harwich

BARKER, ROSALIN. 'Comparing demographic experience: Harwich and Whitby, 1750-1800', *Local population studies* **46**, 1991, 32-49. Based on parish registers.

Hatfield Forest

RACKHAM, OLIVER. *The last forest: the story of Hatfield Forest.* J.M. Dent, 1989. Invaluable as a study of what the term 'Forest' actually meant.

Haveringe atte Bower

McINTOSH, MARJORIE KENISTON. *Autonomy and community: the royal manor of Havering, 1200-1500.* Cambridge: Cambridge University Press, 1986.

McINTOSH, MARJORIE KENISTON. *A community transformed: the manor and liberty of Havering 1500-1620* Cambridge: Cambridge University Press, 1991.

McINTOSH, MARJORIE KENISTON. 'Land tenure and population in the royal manor of Havering, Essex, 1251-1352/3', *Economic history review* 2nd series **33**, 1980, 17-31. General history.

McINTOSH, MARJORIE KENISTON. 'Money lending on the periphery of London, 1300-1600', *Albion* **20**, 1988, 557-71. Study of Havering atte Bower.

SMITH, HAROLD. *A history of the parish of Havering-atte-Bower, Essex.* Colchester: Benham and Company, 1925. Includes notes from many monumental inscriptions, lists of clergy and churchwardens, various lists of subsidy payers, *etc.*

Hinckford Hundred
DYMOND, DAVID. 'The famine of 1527 in Essex', *Local population studies* **26**, 1981, 29-40. Concerns Hinckford Hundred.

Horndon
TINWORTH, W.W. *Saffron, cider and honey: a town trail of Horndon on the Hill.* The author, 1984/5. Mentions many names and includes lists of clergy and publishers of the 'Bell'.

Kelvedon
KENTISH, B.L. *Kelvedon and its antiquities.* Phillimore and Co., 1974. Includes subsidy 1608, hearth tax 1663, rental 1618, pedigrees of Leapingwell and Marler, *etc.*
SHARPE, J.A. 'Crime and delinquency in an Essex parish 1600-1640', in COCKBURN, J.S. ed. *Crime in England, 1550-1800.* Methuen, 1977, 90-109. Based on Archdeaconry court records relating to Kelvedon Easterford.

Laindon
See Stifford

Leyton
KENNEDY, JOHN. *A history of the parish of Leyton, Essex.* Leyton: Phelp Brothers, 1894. Includes lists of clergy and churchwardens, extracts from parish registers and churchwardens, accounts, *etc.*

Leytonstone
HAMMOCK, W.G. *Leytonstone and its history, with special reference to the establishment and development of the church, services therein, and a short account of former residents and residences, etc.* Batten and Davies, 1904.

Little Thurrock
BENTON, TONY. *Boldly from the marshes: a history of Little Thurrock and its people.* The author/Thurrock Museum, 1991.
See also Stifford

Loughton
WALLER, WILLIAM CHAPMAN. *Loughton in Essex.* Epping: Alfred B. Davis, 1899-1900. Pt.1. Collections illustrative of the history of the manor and parish. Pt.2. Transcripts and abstracts of some old wills relating to Loughton.

POHL, DONALD J. *Loughton 1851: the village and its people: a reconstruction based on the 1851 tithe map and award.* Transactions/Chigwell and Loughton History Society **4**. 1988.
DARE, EDWIN H. 'A social initiative in Loughton, Essex; the Loughton Mutual Labor-Aid Society 1891-1899', *Local historian* **24**(4), 1994, 229-42.

Maldon
HUGHET, LEONARD. *A guide to the church of All Saints, Maldon, with outlines of its history, and appendices chiefly of original documents and authorities.* Malson: Gowers, 1909. Includes monumental inscriptions, extracts from borough chamberlains accounts, 15-17th c., list of vicars, *etc.*
PETCHEY, W.J. *A prospect of Maldon 1500-1689.* E.R.O. publication **113**. 1991. Extensive; includes lists of 'high officers' of the borough, and of MPs' 1504-1688.
WALTER, JOHN. 'Grain riots and popular attitudes to the law: Maldon and the crisis of 1629', in BREWER, JOHN & STYLES, JOHN. *An ungovernable people: the English and their law in the 17th and 18th centuries.* Hutchinson, 1980, 47-84.

Mersea
TABOR, MARGARET. 'Marsh marriage', *E.J.* **4**(4), 1969, 215-21. Study of bigamous marriages in Mersea area.

Moreton
DAVEY, CLAIRE. 'A note on mobility in an Essex parish in the early nineteenth century', *Local population studies* **41**, 1988, 61-6. Based on Moreton parish registers.

Mucking
See Stifford

Newport
NURSE, BERNARD. 'Occupations in parish registers: the evidence from Newport, Essex', *Local population studies* **52**, 1994, 39-42.

Orsett
See Stifford

Pleshey

GOUGH, R. *The history and antiquities of Pleshy in the County of Essex.* J. Nichols & Son, 1803. Includes deed abstracts, *etc.*

Ramsden Bellhouse

GIBSON, E.P. *The annals of Ramsden Bellhouse. A short account of the parish of Ramsden Bellhouse in the County of Essex.* ed. F.W. Austen. Chelmsford: H.G. Shergold, 1927. Includes brief extracts from the register and other parish records.

Rochford Hundred

BENTON, PHILIP. *The history of Rochford Hundred (together with the parishes comprised within the union), from former authors, ancient manuscripts, and church registers, treating upon various subjects, including notices of churches and chapels, the clergy, biography and genealogy of families, traditions, superstitions, agriculture, tithe apportionments, and various other matters.* 3 vols. Rochford: A. Harrington, 1867-86. Facsimile reprint, incorporating a companion volume, Southend-on-Sea: Unicorn Press, 1991. Parochial survey.

Stanford le Hope

See Stifford

Stanway

P., A. 'Notices of Stanway, in the Hundred of Lexden, Essex', *Collectanea topographica et genealogica* 7, 1841, 273-8.

Stifford

DEAN, DOREEN, & STUDD, PAMELA. *The Stifford saga, 1180-1980.* Privately printed, 1980. Includes extracts from parish records, outline pedigrees of Lathum, *etc.*

PALIN, W.M. *Stifford and its neighbourhood, past and present.* Taylor and Co., 1871. Primarily a historical survey of 14 neighbouring parishes. Supplemented by PALIN, WILLIAM. *More about Stifford and its neighbourhood, past and present ...* Taylor and Co., 1872.

Stock

JARVIS, L. DONALD. *Stock, Essex: a brief historical survey of the village.* F.R. Bevan, 1934. Includes brief extracts from the parish register.

Stondon Massey

CHANCELLOR, FRED. 'Essex churches XXI: St. Peter and St. Paul, Stondon Massey', *E. Rev.* 7, 1898, 139-55. Includes descent of manor, notes on inscriptions, list of rectors, *etc.*

Tendring Hundred

WATSON, J. YELLOLY. *The Tendring Hundred in the olden time: a series of sketches.* Colchester: Benham and Co., 1877. Parochial survey.

Terling

WRIGHTSON, KEITH. & LEVINE, DAVID. *Poverty and piety in an English village: Terling, 1525-1700.* [Rev. ed.] Oxford: Clarendon Press, 1995. Important modern study.

LEVINE, DAVID. *Family formation in an age of nascent capitalism.* Academia Press, 1977. Study of 19th c. demography in Shepshed and Battesford, Leicestershire, Terling, Essex, and Colyton, Devon.

WRIGHTSON, KEITH. 'Kinship in an English village: Terling, Essex, 1500-1700', in SMITH, RICHARD M., ed. *Land, kinship and life-cycle.* Cambridge: C.U.P., 1984, 313-32.

WRIGHTSON, KEITH. 'Aspects of social differentiation in rural England, c.1580-1660', *Journal of peasant studies* 5(1), 1977, 33-7. General study of Terling, based partly on the parish register.

SPENCE, JEANNETTE. 'Did your ancestors come from Terling?', *E.F.H.* 37, 1985, 21-3; 38, 1985, 16. Brief note on Terling history, including list of 17thc. wills.

Thorpe le Soken

WOOD, ERNEST ALAN. *A history of Thorpe-le-Soken to the year 1890.* T.C. Webb, [1975?] Many names.

West Ham

See East Ham

Willingale Doe

See Braintree

Willingale Spain

See Braintree

Witham

GYFORD, JANET. *Men of bad character: the Witham fires of the 1820s.* Studies in Essex history 1. E.R.O., 1991.

3. BIBLIOGRAPHY AND ARCHIVES.

Published works relating to the history of Essex are innumerable. This volume aims to list those which are of most relevance to genealogists. However, thousands more are listed in a *Victoria County History* volume and its supplement:

POWELL, W.R., ed. *A history of the county of Essex: bibliography.* Oxford University Press for the Institute of Historical Research, 1959.

SAINSBURY, FRANK. *A history of the county of Essex: bibliography supplement.* Oxford University Press for the Institute of Historical Research, 1987.

Two older listing are also available:

MOON, Z. *Essex literature: a catalogue of books published in, or relating to, the County of Essex, to which is added a list of authors who, either by birth or residence, are connected with the county and whose works are in the library.* Leyton: Leyton Public Library, 1900.

WARD, GLADYS A. *Essex local history: a short guide to books and manuscripts.* Witham: National Register of Archives, Essex Committee, 1950.

For theses — which are too often neglected by genealogists — see:

HENNEY, JANICE. *East Anglian studies: theses completed.* Norwich: Centre of East Anglian Studies, 1982.

For a very brief discussion — now very dated — of some important manuscripts, such as the protestation, pollbooks, chartularies, *etc.* see:

ROUND, J.H. 'Some Essex records', *T.E.A.S.* N.S., 15, 1921, 173-8.

Unfortunately there is no general guide to genealogical research in Essex other than those relating to specific institutions. However, if the parishes you are interested in are now suburbs of Greater London, consult:

WEBB, CLIFF. *My ancestors were Londoners: how can I find out more about them?* Society of Genealogists, 1996. Includes information concerning London's Essex suburbs.

See also:

Essex in London: a guide to the records of the London boroughs formerly in Essex deposited in the E.R.O.: Barking and Dagenham; Havering; Newham; Redbridge; Waltham Forest. E.R.O. publications 117. 1992.

Essex Record Office

This is the major archive office for the county, and its holdings have been frequently described in print. The major guide is now:

EMMISON, F.G. *Guide to the Essex Record Office.* 2nd ed. E.R.O. publications 51. 1969. This supersedes two previous works:

EMMISON, F.G. *Guide to the Essex Record Office, part 1: Essex quarter sessions and other official records.* E.R.O. publication 1. 1946.

EMMISON, F.G. *Catalogue of Essex parish records, 1240-1894, with supplement on nonconformist charities, societies and school records, 1341-1903.* 2nd ed. E.R.O. publications 7. 1966.

Every Essex genealogist will need to consult:

Essex family history: a genealogists guide to the Essex Record Office. E.R.O. publication 122. 1993. Extensive listing of a wide range of sources.

The former county archivist, F.G. Emmison, regularly published brief descriptions and histories of the record office. These are listed here by date of publication.

EMMISON, F.G. 'Local archives of Great Britain, II: The Essex Record Office', *Archives* 1(2), 1949, 8-16.

EMMISON, F.G. *The Essex Record Office 1938-1949: a report ...* E.R.O. publications 10. 1950. History of the collection.

EMMISON, F.G. *Archives for all: the Essex Record Office, 1950-1955.* E.R.O. Publications 28. 1956.

EMMISON, F.G. *Royal progress: the Essex Record Office, 1956-61, a report ...* E.R.O. Publications 37. 1962.

EMMISON, F.G. *Record retrospect: the Essex Record Office 1938-63. A report ...* E.R.O. Publications 42. 1964.

See also:
NEWTON, K.C. 'The Essex Record Office in new surroundings', *Journal of the Society of Archivists* **3**, 1965-9, 29-30.
GRAY, V. 'Record office review: Essex', *Family Tree Magazine* **2**(3), 1986, 18.
EMMISON, F.G. 'Essex Record Office accessions', *T.E.A.S.* N.S., **22**, 1940, 361-3; **23**, 1942-5, 181-91 & 361-8.
EMMISON, F.G. 'Essex Record Office: documents received ...', *E. Rev.* **49-60**, 1940-51, *passim.*
A number of works discuss indexes in Essex Record Office:
EMMISON, F.G. 'Needle-searching or spoon-feeding ?', *Journal of the Society of Archivists* **1**(3), 1956, 75-9. Indexes in Essex Record Office.
EMMISON, F.G. 'Essex genealogical indexes: a million references to personal names', *Genealogists magazine* **21**(2), 1983, 55-9. Lists indexes in print and manuscript at Essex Record Office.
STEER, FRANCIS W. Essex Record Office: supplementary list of indexes to personal names', *Genealogists magazine* **10**(15), 1946, 14. Brief list.
For a brief note on name lists at Essex Record Office, see:
HOWELL, E.T. 'Miscellaneous name lists for Essex, 1718-1862,' *E.F.H.* **80**, 1996, 29-30.

Essex Archaeological Society
ESSEX ARCHAEOLOGICAL SOCIETY. *Catalogue of books, pamphlets, periodicals, manuscripts and scrap collections in the library of the Essex Archaeological Society.* Colchester: Benham and Company, 1923.

Essex Society for Family History
HODGE, ELAINE. 'Guest Society: the Essex Society for Family History', *Family Tree Magazine* **8**(11), 1992, 29.

Local Bibliography, Libraries, Archives, etc.

Barking
LOCKWOOD, H.H. *Sources and development of local historical studies in the Barking and Ilford areas.* [Ilford]: Ilford and District History Society, 1973. Published as the society's *transactions* **1**. Review essay.

Billericay
GRANT, WYNFORD. *Billericay bibiography, including details of 150 books and articles about Billericay, and biographies of famous inhabitants of Billericay.* Billericay history series. Billericay: W.P. Grant, 1963.

Dagenham
Essex and Dagenham: a catalogue of books, pamphlets and maps. 2nd ed. Dagenham: Borough of Dagenham Public Libraries, 1961.

Ilford
See Barking

Newham
Guide to the Local Studies Library. London Borough of Newham, [198-?] Includes brief summary of resources.
Resources for family history in the Reference and Local Studies Department. London Borough of Newham Library Services, [198-?] Guide to resources at Stratford.
'The London Borough of Newham', *C.A.* **15**, 1982, 5-8. List of records and locations.

Redbridge
A catalogue of local history documents. London Borough of Redbridge, Libraries Department, 1977.

Romford
'Romford Family History Centre', *Roots in the Forest: the journal of the Waltham Forest Family History Society* **7**(3), 1995, 52-3. Brief note on a local Latter Day Saints.

Thurrock
SPARKES, I.G. *The history of Thurrock: a guide and bibliography.* Upminster: the author, 1960. Includes listings of books and original sources for Alveley, Bulphan, Chadwell St. Mary, Corringham, Dunton, East Tilbury, Fobbing, Grays Thurrock, Horndon on the Hill, Langdon Hills, Little Thurrock, Murking, Orsett, Purfleet, South Ockendon, Stanford Le Hope, Stifford, Tilbury, West Thurrock and West Tilbury.

Walthamstow

HANSON, S.D. *A Walthamstow bibliography.*
Walthamstow Antiquarian Society
occasional publication **12**. 1971
'Lesser known sources to investigate', *Roots
in the Forest: the journal of the Waltham
Forest Family History Society* **6**(7), 1993,
132-4. Lists archives, libraries, museums,
etc. within 10 miles of Walthamstow.

Woodford

'Woodford records at the Passmore Edwards
Museum', *C.A.* **16**, 1982, 6.

Antiquaries' Collections

The collections of manuscripts and notes
made by antiquaries in the nineteenth
century and earlier frequently contain
valuable genealogical information. A number
of these collections have been described in
print:

RICKWORD, G. 'The Elliot heraldic mss.',
T.E.A.S. N.S., **16**, 1923, 50-52. Description
of an antiquarian's collection held by the
Essex Archaeological Society.

LAVER, HENRY. 'The King bequest', *T.E.A.S.*
N.S., **5**, 1895, 65-8. List of an antiquary's
collection of notes held by the Essex
Archaeological Society.

KING, H.W. 'The Morant and Astle mss. and
other historical and topographical
collections relating to Essex', *T.E.A.S.* **2**,
1863, 147-54. Brief discussion of
antiquaries collections.

NEWTON, K.C. 'Some original documents in
the Morant mss.', *T.E.A.S.* 3rd series 2(3),
1970, 289-98. Calendar of various medieval
deeds from an antiquary's collection.

4. PERIODICALS

The major journal for Essex genealogists is:
The Essex family historian. Essex Society for
Family History, 1974- . This is indexed in:
*Index to Essex family historian volumes
1-27.* [ ]: E.S.F.H., [198-?] Further indexes
cover vols. 28-50 and 51-60.
See also:
*Waltham Forest Family History Society
newsletter.* 1978-1983. Continued by: *Roots
in the Forest: the journal of Waltham
Forest Family History Society.* 1984- .
The major historical journal for the county,
which contains many articles of interest to
genealogists is:
*Transactions of the Essex Archaeological
Society.* 1858-1971. Continued by: *Essex
archaeology and history: the transactions
of the Essex Archaeological Society.*
1972- . The first volume under the new
title is designated vol. 4 (third series).
These transactions are indexed in:
SMITH, CHARLOTTE FELL. *General Index to
the transactions of the Essex
Archaeological Society, vols. I-V, 1858-
1895, and vols. I-V, new series. 1878-1895.*
Colchester: [ ], 1900. Not seen.
*General index to the Transactions of the
Essex Archaeological Society volumes VI-
XV, new series, 1896-1920.* Colchester: the
Society, 1926.
Other county wide journals containing
relevant material include:
*The East Anglian, or, notes and queries on
subjects connected with the counties of
Suffolk, Cambridge, Essex and Norfolk.* 4
13 vols. Lowestoft: S. Tymms; London:
Whitaker & Co., 1858-71. New series, 1885-
1910. Each volume has its own index to
persons, places and subjects, except that
only subjects are indexed from N.S. 7-.
L'ESTRANGE, JOHN. *Eastern Counties
collectanea, being notes and queries on
subjects relating to the counties of
Norfolk, Suffolk, Essex and Cambridge.*
Norwich: Thomas R. Tallack, 1872-3.
*The Essex review: an illustrated quarterly
record of everything of permanent
interest in the county.* Chelmsford:
Edmund Durrant & Co., 1892-1956/7.
Indexed in:

BENHAM, W. GURNEY. *General index to the Essex review, volume I (1892) to the end of volume XXXVI (1927).* Colchester: Benham & Company, 1930.

WALKER, KENNETH. *General index to the Essex review volume XXXVII, 1928, to LXI, 1952.* Colchester: Benham and Company, 1953. A typescript index covering 1953-7 is also available.

Essex journal: a quarterly journal for the county of Essex. [ ]: Essex Archaeological and Historical Congress, 1966- . Incorporates *Essex review*.

Home counties magazine, devoted to the topography of London, Middlesex, Essex, Herts., Bucks., Berks., Surrey, and Kent. 14 vols. F.E. Robinson & Co., 1899-1912. Indexed in *Home counties magazine: general index to volumes I-X.* G. Bell & Sons, [1911?]

Local Historical Journals
In addition to those journals which cover the whole county, there are also a number of local historical periodicals, which are listed here.

Benfleet
Journal of the Benfleet and District Historical Society. 1956-82.

Chingford
Chingford Antiquarian and Historical Society bulletin. 1958-78. 11 issues.
Chingford notes Chingford: Chingford Historical Society, 1975- . Newsletter.

Colchester
Colchester Archaeological Group quarterly bulletin. 1958- . Became *annual* from **14,** 1971.

Ingatestone
Ingatestone and Freyerning Historical and Archaeological Society transactions. 1966 - . Little of genealogical interest.

Newham
Newham History Society newsletter. 1988- . Little of genealogical relevance.

Rochford
Rochford historian. Rochford Hundred Historical Society, 1968- . Little of genealogical interest.

Romford
Romford record. [Romford]: Romford and District Historical Society, 1968-84.

Saffron Walden
Saffron Walden history: the occasional journal of the Saffron Walden Antiquarian Society. 1972- .

Southend
Transactions of the Southend-on-Sea & District Antiquarian & Historical Society. 1921- .

Thurrock
The Thurrock Local History Society journal. 1956-66. Continued as *Panorama: the journal of the Thurrock Local History Society* 1967-. Indexed in: *Panorama: index vols. 1-20. Thurrock Local History Society journal 1956-1977.* 1980. A further index covering vols. 21-30, 1978 - 1989 was published in 1992.

Wanstead
Wanstead Historical Society journal. 1983 -. Little of genealogical interest.

Woodford
Woodford and District Antiquarian Society proceedings and transactions. 1933-68. Title varies.

5. OCCUPATIONAL SOURCES

Many works provide biographical information on persons of particular occupations. Here, the term 'occupation' is used broadly, encompassing men with particular statuses, e.g. freemasons, as well. The works listed here generally contain information of relevance to genealogists; historical accounts of paricular occupations which do not include names or references to useful sources are not listed. For clergymen, see section 13, Members of Parliament, justices of the peace, sherrifs *etc.,* section 11, and teachers and students, section 15. This list complements the listing in Raymond's *Occupational Sources for genealogists.*

Architects
BETTLEY, JAMES. 'A checklist of Essex architects',1834-1914', *E.A.H.* **24**, 1993, 168-84.

Authors
HEFFER, R. 'Saffron Walden local authors and authoresses', *E.Rev.* **24**, 1915, 126-30. See also 192-6. Biographical notes.

Bankers
PRESTON, HAROLD, *Early East Anglian banks and bankers.* Thetford: Harold Preston, 1995. Includes list, naming partners, 18-19th c.

CHRISTY, MILLER. *The history of banks and banking in Essex.* [ ], 1906. Reprinted from *The journal of the Institute of Bankers* 1906, 319-30.

Clockmakers
HEAPS, JAMES. *Essex clock and watchmakers.* Billericay: Heron Jader, 1979. List.

MASON, BERNARD. *Clock and watchmaking in Colchester, England: a history of provincial clockmaking from the fifteenth to the nineteenth centuries in the oldest recorded town in Great Britain.* Country Life, 1969.

NEWMAN, HOWARD C. 'Time passed', *Saffron Walden history* **5**(40), 1990, 164-7. Notes on clock and watchmakers of Saffron Walden, with list.

SIER, L.C. 'Colchester and other clock and watchmakers', *E.Rev.* **48**, 1939, 4-9. Lists 39 names, 1639-1826.

Clothworkers
HOPE, T.M. 'Essex clothworkers, 1636-7', *T.E.A.S.* N.S., **23**, 1945-7, 177-8. Includes list of Bocking clothiers in 1636.

Convicts
'List compiled from the returns of convicts held on prison hulks in the quarter ended 31st March 1851', *E.F.H.* **53**, 1989, 16-18. List of Essex convicts.

DANIEL, R.A. 'Back to the prison hulks: list compiled from the returns of convicts held on prison hulks quarter ended 31 March 1841', *E.F.H.* **58**, 1990, 50-52; **54**, 1991, 50. Lists convicts mainly from Chelmsford.

'Even more on hulks returns', *E.F.H.* **71**, 1994, 33-5. Lists Essex convicts on hulks at Portsmouth, 1851.

Cotton Workers
EMMISION, F.G. 'Essex children deported to a Lancashire cotton mill, 1799', *E.Rev.* **53**, 1944, 77-85. Discussion of ten apprenticeship indentures relating to children sent to Pendleton.

Cricketers
NEWNHAM, LESLIE. *Essex county cricket, 1876-1975: a brief history.* Colchester: Vineyard Press, 1976. Includes a 'register of Essex county cricketers, 1876-1975'.

Firemen
FARMER, JACK. *Epping Town Fire Brigade: a history.* Waltham Abbey: Epping Forest District Museum, 1983.

Foresters
WALLER, WILLIAM CHAPMAN. 'The foresters' walks in Waltham Forest', *E.Rev.* **14**, 1905, 193-203. Extracts from returns of slain deer, late 17th c., with names of keepers, recipients, *etc.*

Freemasons
GOUGH, C. *History of the Chigwell Lodge no.453: 1838-1914.* Chigwell: The Lodge, 1914. Includes list of members.

'Freemasons in Thurrock', *Panorama: the journal of the Thurrock Local History Society* **24**, 1980, 61-3. List, 1797-1817.

Gypsies

THOMPSON, T.W. 'Youngs, Gibsons and their associates, an enquiry into the origin of certain East Anglian and metropolitan gypsy families', *Gypsy Lore Society journal* 24, 1945, 44-56; 25, 1946, 39-45. Of Norfolk, Suffolk and Essex.

Innkeepers

EDWARDS, F.C. 'Licensed houses in Harlow', *E.Rev.* 21, 1912, 31-8. Lists innkeepers.
RICKWORD, GERALD O. 'The Red Lion at Colchester: the early days of an ancient hostelry', *E.Rev.* 48, 1939, 39-43. Identifies innkeepers, 16th c.
THOMAS, JANE, & HOLDER, LINDA. 'The story of the Golden Lion', *Romford record* 3, 1970, 9-25. Romford public house. Identifies innkeepers 16-20th c.
SMITH, C. FELL. 'Essex inns', *E.Rev.* 11, 1902, 117-8. Lists innkeepers, 1636.

Land Surveyors

MASON, A. STUART. *Essex on the map: the 18th century land surveyors of Essex.* E.R.O. publication 105. 1990.

Medical Practitioners

RADCLIFFE, WALTER. 'The Colchester Medical Society, 1774', *Medical history* 20, 1976, 394-401.

Merchants

GIRLING, F.A. 'Essex merchants' marks' *Colchester Archaeological Group quarterly bulletin* 3(2), 1960, 28-30. Lists 20 marks, mostly from tombs or carved on houses.

Millers

BENHAM, HERVEY. *Some Essex water mills.* Colchester: Essex County Newspapers, 1976. Many names of millers.
FARRIES, K.G. *Essex windmills, millers and millwrights.* 5 vols. Charles Skilton, 1981-5. v.1. An historical review. v.2. A technical review. v.3-5. A review by parishes. Many names, especially in the parish review volumes.

Milliners

D'CRUZE, SHANI. 'To acquaint the ladies: women traders in Colchester c.1750-c.1800', *Local historian* 17, 1986, 156-61. Brief notes on milliners.

Naturalists

WARD, BERNARD T. 'Some Essex naturalists', *Essex naturalist* 29, 1956, 306-26.

Oystermen

BENHAM, HERVEY, et al. *Essex gold: the fortunes of the Essex oysterman.* E.R.O. publication 120. 1993.

Painters

DAY, HAROLD A.E. *East Anglian painters.* 3 vols. Eastbourne: Eastbourne Fine Arts, 1968-9. Includes biographical notes; covers Essex, Suffolk and Norfolk.

Passengers

WATSON, PETER. 'Drown'd in the Northfleet', *West Middlesex Family History Society journal* 12(4), 1994, 7-12. Includes list of 342 passengers aboard the Northfleet, which went down off Dungeness in 1873, having sailed from East India Docks.

Patentees

RAMSEY, A.R.J. 'The early Essex patents for inventions', *E.Rev.* 56, 1947, 15-22, 75-83 & 113-22. List of patentees.

Photographers

APPLEBY, DAVID & APPLEBY, JOHN. *The magic boxes: professional photographers & their studios in North Essex 1845-1937.* E.R.O. Publication 115. 1992. Includes 'a directory of photographic studios and professional photographers in North Essex, 1845-1937.

Pipe Makers

GANT, LEONARD H. 'Clay tobacco pipe makers: a Colchester chronology', *Colchester Archaeological Group bulletin* 2, 1959, 3-4. Brief introduction; no names.

Policemen

The history of police in Essex is outlined in:
SCOLLAN, MAUREEN. *Sworn to serve: police in Essex 1840-1990.* Phillimore, 1994. Includes list of recruits, 1840-1900.
WOODGATE, JOHN. *The Essex police.* Lavenham: Terence Dalton, 1985. Detailed study, but few names.

There are two articles on sources for Essex policemen:

FEATHER, FRED. 'One hundred and fifty years: some Essex police records for the use of genealogists', *E.F.H.* **53**, 1989, 10-11.

CROSS, AVRIL. 'What's in it for the family historian? : Essex Police Museum',*Family tree magazine* **12**(1), 1995, 54-5. The museum has personnel records.

Local studies include:

ELLIOT, BRIAN. *A history of Loughton and Chigwell police.* Chigwell and Loughton Historical Society 1992. Published as the society's *transactions* **5**.

PLEYDELL, PETER J.E. 'The special constabulary in Walthamstow (1940-43)', *Journal of the Police History Society* **8**, 1993, 71-80.

Postmen

Articles on Essex postmen are regularly published in:
Essex post: Essex Postal History Society bulletin 1965-.

Local studies include:

HEELEY D. 'Postmasters of Ingatestone', *Ingatestone and Freyerning Historical and Archaeological Society transactions* **17**, 1979, 13-14. List, 17-19th c.

BENTON, G. MONTAGU. 'The postal services at Saffron Walden in the nineteenth century', *E.Rev.* **56**, 1947, 23-8. Identifies postmasters, *etc.*

TRINDER, J.F. *The postal history of the Tendring Hundred of Essex* Clacton: J.F. Trinder, 1971. Includes names of postmasters.

Seamen

WAKELING, A.L. *Stories behind the tiles.* Brightlingsea: Scribe Publishing, 1973. Notes on tiles commemorating Brightlingsea men lost at sea, 1883-1935.

Servants

FOLEY, B.C. '1760: yearly wages of Lord Petre's servants', *E.Rev.* **2**, 1960, 30-31. Lists servants.

Shipbuilders

BANBURY, PHILIP. *Shipbuilders of the Thames and Medway.* Newton Abbot: David and Charles, 1971.

Smugglers

BENHAM, HERVEY. *The smugglers' century: the story of smugglers on the Essex coast, 1730-1830.* E.R.O. Publication **94**. 1986.

Soldiers, Militiamen *etc.*

With the exception of the present generation, most Englishmen have served in the armed forces. For Essex, most of the published literature deals with the two world wars; however, for two brief articles on earlier periods, see:

CLARK, ANDREW. 'The Essex territorial force in 1608',*E.Rev.* **17**, 1908, 98-115. See also **18**, 1909, 65-74. Includes names of captains.

CHASE, MALCOLM S. 'Artillery volunteers at Grays 1860-1908', *Panorama: the journal of the Thurrock Historical Society* **21**, 1977/8, 65-70. Lists 17 volunteers.

Memorials

There are many memorials, *etc.,* to soldiers who lost their lives in the two world wars. See:

IMPERIAL WAR GRAVES COMMISSION. *The war dead of the Commonwealth: the register of the names of those who fell in the Great War and are buried in cemeteries and churchyards in North and Central Essex, 1914-1918.* The Commission, 1931. Reprinted with amendments. Maidenhead: Commonwealth War Graves Commission, 1988.

HUNT, EDGAR A., ed. *The Colchester war memorial souvenir.* Colchester: Essex Telegraph, 1923. Includes honours list, roll of honour, and list of fallen.

Roll of men from Southend-on-Sea and district who fell for their country in the Great War 1914-19. Southend-on-Sea: John H. Burrows & Sons, 1920.

COMMONWEALTH WAR GRAVES COMMISSION. *The war dead of the Commonwealth: the register of the names of those who fell in the 1939-45 war and are buried in cemeteries and churchyards in the County of Essex.* 3 vols. Commonwealth War Graves Commission, 1961.

Soldiers, Militiamen, etc. continued

Regimental and Unit Histories

There are a variety of histories of particular regiments etc., not all of which are listed here. Only those works which have lists of names, such as rolls of honour, or other works likely to be of interest to genealogists, are identified here.

East Essex Regiment of Foot

CARTER, THOMAS. *Historical record of the Forty-Fourth, or the East Essex Regiment of Foot.* 2nd ed. Chatham: Gale & Polden, 1887. Includes various lists of officers and men.

Essex Gentlemen and Yeomanry Cavalry

CRANMER-BYNG, J.L. 'Essex prepares for invasion 1796-1805', *E.Rev.* **60,** 1951, 127-34 & 185-93; **61,** 1952, 43-7 & 57-74. Includes muster roll of the 4th Troop of Essex Gentlemen and Yeomanry Cavalry.

Essex Home Guard

FINCH, PETER. *Warmen courageous: the story of the Essex Home Guard.* Southend-on-Sea: John H. Burrows & Sons, 1951. Includes various names.

Essex Militia

BURROWS, JOHN WM. *The Essex Militia.* Essex units in the war, 1914-1919 4. Southend: John H. Burrows & Sons, 1929. Includes lists of officers.

Essex Regiment

BURROWS, JOHN WM. *The Essex Regiment: Essex Territorial Infantry Brigade, (4th, 5th, 6th and 7th Battalions) also 8th (cyclists) Battalion the Essex Regiment.* Essex units in the war 1914-1919, 5. Southend: J.H. Burrows & Sons, [1932]. Includes lists of officers, honours, etc.

Soldiers died in the Great War 1914-19. Part 48. The Essex Regiment. H.M.S.O., 1921. Reprinted Polstead: J.B. Hayward & Sons, 1989.

The Distinguished Conduct Medal 1914-20 citation: the Essex Regiment. London Stamp Exchange, [198-].

Essex Yeomanry

BURROWS, JOHN WM. *The Essex Yeomanry, containing also a short account of military activity in the country during the Napoleonic war.* The Essex Yeomanry 3. Southend: John H. Burrows & Sons, 1925. Includes list of war honours and casualties, 1914-18.

PARKER, R.C.O. *The Essex Yeomanry who's who.* [ ], 1950.

1/4th Essex

BECKETT, DENIS. *1/4th Essex: a battalion of the Eighth Army.* Wilson & Whitworth, [1945.] Includes roll of honour, 1939-45.

1/5th Essex

GIBBONS, T. *With the 1/5th Essex in the East.* Colchester: Benham and Company, 1921. Includes lists of casualties, honours and awards, and officers.

10th Royal Hussars

WHITMORE, F.H.D.C. *The 10th (P.W.O.) Royal Hussars and the Essex Yeomanry during the European War, 1914-1918.* Colchester: Benham and Company, 1920. Includes various appendices listing officers and men.

17th Light Anti-Aircraft Regiment

EELES, H.S. *The history of the 17th Light Anti Aircraft Regiment, Royal Artillery, 1938-1945.* Tunbridge Wells: Courier Co., 1946. Includes various lists of names.

Steam Engine Builders

CLARK, RONALD H. *Steam-engine builders of Suffolk, Essex and Cambridgeshire.* Norwich: Augustine Steward Press, 1950.

Surveyors.

BRIGGS, NANCY. 'The evolution of the office of county surveyor in Essex 1700-1816', *Architectural history* **27,** 1984, 297-307.

Tradesmen

In an age when currency was in short supply, tradesmen frequently issues their own tokens. Studies of these frequently reveal information of genealogical interest.

See:
ADAMS, STUART JOHN. *The Essex collection of post 1820 tokens, tallies and medallions.* Hornchurch: Havering Numismatic Society, 1990. v.1. only issued.
COXALL, JOHN. *The Walthamstow tokens.* Official publication **18**. Walthamstow: Walthamstow Antiquarian Society, 1927.
GILBERT, WILLIAM. 'The token coinage of Essex in the seventeenth century', *T.E.A.S.* N.S., **13**, 1915, 184-99 & 267-80; **14**, 1918, 1-15 & 146-57; **17**, 1926, 242-56. See also **17**, 1926, 130-31; **18**, 1928, 73 & 143.
JUDSON, EILEEN. *The lives and wills of Essex token issuers, incorporating a re-listing of the seventeenth century trade tokens of Essex.* Little Bardfield: [the author], 1987.
JUDSON, EDWARD & JUDSON, EILEEN. *Re-listing of the seventeenth century trade tokens of Essex.* Little Bardfield: [the authors], 1973.
MASON, ERNEST N. *Ancient tokens of Colchester.* Colchester: Benham and Co., 1902. Tradesmen's tokens.
MACFARLANE, ALAN. *Witchcraft in Tudor and Stuart England: a regional and comparative study.* Routledge & Kegan Paul, 1970. Based on Essex records.

Witches
EWEN, C. L ESTRANGE. ed. *Witch hunting and witch trials: the indictments for witchcraft from records of 1373 assizes held for the Home Circuit, 1559-1736.* Kegan Paul, Trench, Trubner & Co., 1929. Evidence from Essex, Kent, Hertfordshire, Surrey and Sussex.
HAINING, PETER, ed. *The witchcraft papers: contemporary records of the witchcraft hysteria in Essex, 1560-1700.* Robert Hale & Company, 1974. Includes depositions, etc., of witnesses.
MACFARLANE, ALAN. *Witchcraft in Tudor and Stuart England: a regional and comparative Study.* Routledge & Keegan Paul, 1970. Based on Essex records.

6. PARISH REGISTERS AND OTHER RECORDS OF BIRTHS, MARRIAGES AND DEATHS

Parish registers are vital sources for the genealogist. The standard guide to Essex registers is:
WILCOX, ANTHONY. *National index of parish registers: a guide to Anglican, Roman Catholic and nonconformist registers, together with information on bishops transcripts, modern copies and marriage licences, volume 9, part 4: Essex.* Society of Genealogists, 1993.
Registers — and much else — held by Essex Record Office are listed in:
Essex family history: a genealogists guide to the Essex Record Office. 5th ed. E.R.O. publication **122**. 1996. This supersedes:
ESSEX RECORD OFFICE. *A handlist of parish and nonconformist registers in the Essex Record Office, 1982-3.* E.R.O. publication **86**. 1982.
For registers from Essex's suburban fringe, see:
GRAHAM, N.H. *The genealogists consolidated guide to parish registers in the Outer London area, 1538 to 1837.* 3rd ed. Petts Wood: the author, 1984.
GUILDHALL LIBRARY. *Handlist of parish registers, part two: registers and register transcripts of Anglican churches and chapels in Greater London, outside the City.* 5th ed. Guildhall Library, 1986.
HARRIS, T.C. *Guide to parish registers deposited in the Greater London Record Office.* 2nd ed. Greater London Record Office, 1991. Lists a few items relating to metropolitan Essex.
See also the now out-dated:
BOYDEN, PETER B. *A catalogue of transcripts of Essex parish registers and monumental inscriptions.* Colchester: Essex Archaeological Society, 1980.
TANCOCK, O.W. 'Essex parish register books', *E.Rev.* **7**, 1896, 176-84; **8**, 1897, 13-19 & 202-14; **9**, 1900, 161-9; **10**, 1901, 36-42 & 143-9. List of surviving registers.
Parish registers indexed in an important baptismal index are listed in:

25

NUTT, J. 'Essex baptism index', *E.F.H.* **83**, 1997, 50-52; **84**, 1997, 22-4. Lists parishes indexed.

Registers at Grays and Redbridge are listed in two brief articles (now both out-dated):

CATTY, MERYL. 'Central Reference Library, Grays, Essex', *E.F.H.* **18**, 1980, 10-12. List of parish registers on microfilm, etc.

'Redbridge source material', *C.A.* **9**, 1981, 13-19. List of printed and typescript transcripts of registers at Redbridge local history collection.

'Stray' entries from non-Essex parish registers are listed in a number of works:

'Hampshire strays in Essex', *Hampshire family historian* **11**(2), 1984, 80-82. Brief list from parish registers.

BULLEN, R. FREEMAN. 'East Anglian marriages in the church of St. Botolph, Bishopsgate', *E.A.M.* 1913, 49 & 52. Mainly Essex.

BULLEN, R. FREEMAN. 'East Anglian marriages in Stepney registers', *E.A.M.* **1911**, *passim.* Strays from Norfolk, Suffolk, Essex and Cambridgeshire, 1581-1719.

NOLAN, N.M. 'Register of the Catholic Chapels Royal, and of the Portuguese Embassy Chapel, 1662-1829: marriages', *E.Rec.* **17**, 1975, 28-32. Essex extracts.

RATCLIFFE, RICHARD. 'Some Lincolnshire Regiment (10th Foot) marriages in Essex', *Lincolnshire Family History Society [magazine]* **1** (3), 1990, 50. Lists 9 marriages.

SHANAHAN, D. 'Catholic marriage 1837-1870', *E.Rec.* **20**, 1878, 34-8. Essex strays.

ANSTRUTHER, GODFREY. 'Some more Essex marriages', *E.Rec.* **20**, 1978, 75.

'Essex entries in Suffolk parish registers', *E.Rev.* **61**, 1952, 96.

GLASSCOCK, J.L. 'Essex references from the parish register of Bishops Stortford, Herts., 1561-1712', *E.Rev.* **31**, 1922, 75-82.

For non-conformist registers on the fringes of London, see:

'East End nonconformist registers in the Public Record Office', *E.F.H.* **57**, 1990, 12. List.

An index to Catholic marriages in London and Essex is described in:

HUMPHERY-SMITH, CECIL R. 'Catholic marriages', *E.C.A. journal* **2** (4), 1987, 92-3. Description of an index to Catholic marriages in London and Essex.

ANSTRUTHER, GODFREY. 'Index of Catholic marriages', *C.A.* **4**, 1979, 20-21. Discussion of an index covering London, Middlesex and Essex.

An additional or alternative source of information on marriages are the allegation bonds required for the issue of marriage licences. These are described, with discussions of an indexing project, in:

RAYMENT, JOHN L. 'Marriage licences of Essex', *E.F.H.* **56**, 1990, 5-10; **58**, 1990, 3-5.

For allegations in the registry of the Bishop of London (the diocese of London covered most of Essex) see:

GLENCROSS, REGINALD M., ed. *A calendar of the marriage licence allegations in the Registry of the Bishop of London.* Index library **62** & **66**. British Record Society, 1937-40. The diocese included most Essex parishes. Abstracts of many of these allegations are printed in:

ARMYTAGE, GEO. J., ed. *Allegations for marriage licences issued by the Bishop of London 1520 to 1610,* extracted by Joseph Lemuel Chester. Publication of the Harleian Society **25**. 1887. This is continued for 1611 to 1628 in volume **26**. 1887.

For Archdeaconry of Essex marriage allegations, see:

MARSHALL, GERALD. 'Marriage allegations in the court of the Archdeacon of Essex', *East Anglian* N.S. **7**, 1897-8, 289-91. Covers 1691-7 only.

During the Interregnum, the clergy ceased to have responsibility for keeping parish registers. The men appointed to do the job are listed in:

SMITH, HAROLD. 'The registers' of 1654', *E. Rev.* **37**, 1928, 8-16.

Many parish registers have been published or discussed in print. The following list attempts to identify all of these publications. It does not, however, include the many unpublished transcripts which have been made. Bear in mind, too, that publication does not in any way guarantee the accuracy of a transcript: it is still wise to check the original if possible.

Ashdon

BROWN, R.H., & BANHAM, D.B.R., eds. 'Marriages at Ashdon, 1557 to 1812',in PHILLIMORE, W.P.W. ed. *E.P.R.M.* **1.** *P.P.R.S.* **101.** 1909, 103-28.

Aveley

GOODES, AUBREY. 'Aveley parish register books', *E.Rev.* **29,** 1920, 44-5. List.

Barking

KING, H.W. 'Notes on the registers of the parish of Barking', *T.E.A.S.* **2,** 1863, 122-33. Discussion, including some extracts.

Barnston

WARD, CHARLES JAMES. *The evolution of the marriage register traced in the old church records of Barnston parish.* G.J. Palmer & Sons, 1912. General discussion.
'Extracts from the register of Barnston, Co. Essex', *Genealogist* **5,** 1881, 23-5.

Beaumont

CRISP, F.A., ed. *The parish registers of Beaumont, Essex.* Frederick Arthur Crisp, 1899. Baptisms 1565-1678; marriages 1567-1677; burials 1564-1670.

Bobbingworth

CRISP, F.A., ed. *The parish registers of Bobbingworth, Essex.* Frederick Arthur Crisp, 1884. Baptisms 1559-1785; marriages 1559-1753; burials 1563-1785.

Bocking

GOODWIN, J.J. ed. *The first register of St. Mary's church, Bocking, Essex, England.* [ ]: privately printed, 1903. Baptisms 1561-1605; marriages 1593-1639; burials 1558-1628.

Boreham

BROWNE, ROBERT H. 'Parish registers II: Boreham', *E.Rev.* **1,** 1892, 212-23. Includes 1641/2 protestation return and many extracts from the register 1559-1798.

Boxted

PHILLIMORE, W.P.W. & STURT, NEVILLE, eds. 'Marriages at Boxted, 1559 to 1837', in PHILLIMORE, W.P.W., ed. *E.P.R.M.* **1;** *P.P.R.S.* **101,** 1909, 1-30.

Castle Hedingham

'Extracts from parish registers, no. 8: Castle Hedingham, Essex', *East Anglian* **2,** 1886, 33. Brief extracts.

Chelmsford

PHILLIMORE, W.P.W., & BLAGG, THOS. M. eds. *E.P.R.M.* **2.** *P.P.R.S.* **142.** 1912. The whole volume is a transcript of Chelmsford marriages, 1539-1770.
'Marriages at Chelmsford, 1771 to 1837',in ARNOLD-WALLINGER, R.N. ed. *E.P.R.M.* **3.** *P.P.R.S.* **200.** 1913, 1-75.
TANCOCK, O.W. 'An introduction to the earliest parish register book belonging to the cathedral church of St. Mary, Chelmsford', *E.Rev.* **32,** 1923, 182-95. General discussion.
TANCOCK, O.W. 'The old parish register books of the Deanery of Chelmsford', *E.Rev.* **5,** 1869, 163-74. General discussion with list.

Chelmsford Deanery

TANCOCK, O.W. 'The old parish register books of the Deanery of Chelmsford' , *E.Rev.* **5,** 1896, 163-74. General discussion with list.

Chingford

BROWN, R.H. & BROWN, P.M., eds. *Your Chingford ancestors: Baptisms, marriages and burials from 1283 to 1812 taken from bishop's transcripts 1639-40, marriage register 1755-1812, church clerk's copy 1790-1812, monumental inscriptions 1585-1812, national census 1851, wills, 1283-1756, and other miscellaneous records.* Chingford: R.H. & P.M. Brown, 1985.

Colchester

WORRALL, EDW. S. 'Some Essex Catholic registers III: Colchester', *E.Rec.* **10,** 1968 79-81. Description, not a transcript.

Saint Leonard

[CRISP, F.A.], ed. *The parish registers of St. Leonards, Colchester, 1670-71.* Frederick Arthur Crisp, 1885. 21 months only.

Saint Nicholas

GOLDING, CHARLES. 'St. Nicholas, Colchester', *E.Rev.* **7,** 1898, 251-4. Brief extracts from the parish registers, 16-19th c.

Dutch Church

MOENS, W.J.C., ed. *Register of baptisms in the Dutch church at Colchester from 1645 to 1728.* Publications of the Huguenot Society **12.** 1905. Includes many appendices of related documents, e.g. list of strangers, 1571, lay subsidy returns, list of attestations by Huguenots from Colchester in London churches, *etc.*

Crondon Park

LANGTON, FRANCIS A.R., & HANSOM, JOSEPH S., eds. 'The catholic registers of the domestic chapel formerly at Crondon Park, Essex, with some notes relating to Hopar, Lancashire', in *Miscellanea* **5.** Publications of the Catholic Record Society **6.** 1909. 327-63. 18-19th c. Includes extracts from Stock cum Ramsden Bellhouse parish registers, 16-19th c.

Danbury

BROWNE, ROBERT H. 'Parish registers III: Danbury', *E.Rev.* **2,** 1893, 32-5. Brief extracts, 17-18th c.

Debden

'Extracts from parish registers, no. 9: Debden, Co. Essex', *East Anglian* **2** 1866, 53-4. Brief.

Easthorpe

HARRISON, A.D. *Easthorpe records from the parish registers 1572-1812.* Colchester: Acorn Press, 1955. Discussion with some extracts.

Felsted

ROWNTREE, C.BRIGHTWEN. 'Quakers Mount at Bannister Green, Felstead, Essex', *Journal of the Friends History Society* **39,** 1947, 45-8. Extracts from Felstead registers relating to burials of Quakers, 1678-1706.

Fyfield

CRISP, F.A., ed. *The parish registers of Fyfield, Essex, 1538-1700.* F.A. Crisp, 1896.

Great Clacton

GATFIELD, GEORGE. 'The history and preservation of parish registers, with special reference to the register of Great Clacton' , *E.Rev.* **6,** 1897, 215-31. General discussion with a few extracts.

Great Horkesley

STURT, NEVILLE, ed. 'Marriages at Great Horkesley, 1558 to 1836', in PHILLIMORE, W.P.W., ed. *E.P.R.M.* **1**; *P.P.R.S.* **101,** 1909, 31-63.

Great Leighs

CLARK, ANDREW, ed. 'Marriages at Great Leighs 1560 to 1837',in ROEBUCK, G.E., ed. *E.P.R.M.* **4.** *P.P.R.S.* **214.** Phillimore and Co., 1914, 107-32.

CLARK, ANDREW. 'Notes as to Great Leighs registers, 1560-1760', *E.Rev.* **17,** 1908, 91-4. General discussion; no extracts.

Great Wigborough

STEPHENSON, P.A.F., ed. *The parish registers of Great and Little Wigborough in the County of Essex.* Canterbury: Cross and Jackman, 1905. Covers 1586-1812. Includes list of rectors, and monumental inscriptions.

Greenstead

CRISP, F.A. ed. *The parish registers of Greenstead, Essex.* Frederick Arthur Crisp, 1892. For 1561-1812; includes banns 1755-1812.

Halstead

OSBORNE, D. 'Suffolk strays into Halstead, Essex', *Suffolk roots: the journal of the Suffolk Genealogy Society* **5**(1), 1979, 5. For 1620-1753.

SPERLING, C.F.D. 'Some notes on the parish registers of Halstead', *T.E.A.S.* N.S. **5,** 1895, 53-62. Includes brief extracts.

Havering atte Bower

SMITH, HAROLD. 'Havering-atte-Bower registers', *E.Rev.* **25,** 1916, 144-50. General discussion.

High Easter

GEPP, EDWARD. 'The parish register books of High Easter', *E.Rev.* **19,** 1910, 169-80. General description, with a few extracts.

Ilford

LOCKWOOD, HERBERT HOPE. 'Some notes on early 19th century Ilford burials', *C.A.* **63**, 1994, 9. Brief notes on parish registers.

Ingatestone Hall

WORRALL, EDW. W. 'Some Essex Catholic registers, I', *E.Rev.* **5**(3), 1963, 91-3. Notes on the register of Ingatestone Hall, 18-19th

Lambourne

CRISP, F.A. ed. *The parish register of Lambourne, Essex*. Frederick Arthur Crisp, 1890. Baptisms 1582-1709; marriages 1584-1708; burials 1584-1708 and 1788.

Little Heath

'St. James Chapel, Little Heath, 1862-1983/4', *C.A.* **21**, 1983/4, 16-18. Includes index to marriages, 1888-1930.

Little Horkesley

STURT, NEVILLE, ed. 'Marriages at Little Horkesley, 1568 to 1812', in PHILLIMORE, W.P.W., ed. *E.P.R.M.* **1**. *P.P.R.S.* **101**. 1909, 65-79.

Little Leighs

CLARK, A. 'Marriages at Little Leighs', *E.Rev.* **23**, 1914, 179-85. General discussion, with many extracts from the parish register.

CLARK, ANDREW, ed. 'Marriages at Little Leighs, 1680 to 1837', in ROEBUCK, G.E., ed. *E.P.R.M.* **4**; *P.P.R.S.* **214**, 1914, 133-43.

Little Wigborough

See Great Wigborough

Margaret Roding

JOHNSTON, GEORGE HARVEY. 'Baptisms at Margaret Roding, Essex, 1538-87', *Genealogist* **6**, 1890, 12-16; **7**, 1891, 87-90 & 193-6.

JOHNSTON, GEORGE HARVEY. 'Marriages at Margaret Roding, Essex, 1541-1663', *Genealogist* N.S., **9**, 1893, 242-3.

Moreton

CRISP, F.A. ed. *The parish registers of Moreton, Essex*. Frederick Arthur Crisp, 1890. Covers 1558-1759.

Moze

CRISP, F.A., ed. *The parish register of Moze*. Frederick Arthur Crisp, 1899. Baptisms 1551-1678; marriages 1557-1674; burials 1558-1678.

Navestock

'Marriages at Navestock, 1538 to 1812', in PHILLIMORE, W.P.W., ed. *E.P.R.M.* **1**. *P.P.R.S.* **101**. 1909, 129-54.

Nazeing

All Saints church, Nazeing: index 1559-1840. Nazeing: Nazeing Parochial Church Council, 1996. Index to the parish register.

Nevendon

See North Benfleet

Newham

PARK, STEPHEN. *A guide to the parish registers of Newham*. Hornchurch: East of London F.H.S., 1983. Lists records of over 30 churches, with notes on cemeteries.

North Benfleet

SMITH, HAROLD. 'Early registers of North Benfleet and Nevendon', *E.Rev.* **42**, 1933, 62-7.

Ongar

CRISP, F.A., ed. *The parish registers of Ongar, Essex*. Frederick Arthur Crisp, 1886. Baptisms 1558-1750; marriages 1560-1749; burials 1558-1750.

Pebmarsh

BAYLEY, T.D.S. 'Pebmarsh parish registers: how two rectors kept them', *E.Rev.* **54**, 1945, 18-20. General discussion.

Prittlewell

St. Mary's church, Prittlewell, Southend-on-Sea: register of baptisms 1649-1812; register of marriages 1645-1812; register of burials 1645-1812. Southend-on-Sea: John H. Burrows & Sons, 1921.

Ramsden Bellhouse

AUSTEN, F.W. 'Parish registers', *E.Rev.* **54**, 1945, 89-92. Discussion of registers for Ramsden Bellhouse.

See also Crondon Park and Stock

Roxwell

WALLINGER, R.N. ARNOLD, ed. 'Marriages at Roxwell, 1559 to 1837', in ROEBUCK, C.E., ed. *E.P.R.M.* **4**; *P.P.R.S.* **214**. 1914, 73-105.

Stapleford Tawney

CRISP, F.A., ed. *The parish registers of Stapleford Tawney, Essex* Frederick Arthur Crisp, 1892. Covers 1558-1752 (to 1694 for baptisms).

Stifford

CRISP, F.A., ed. *The parish registers of Stifford, Essex.* Frederick Arthur Crisp, 1885. Baptisms 1573-1883; marriages 1572-1753; burials 1572-1783.

Stisted

SMITH, CHARLOTTE FELL. 'Stisted parish registers', *E.Rev.* **15**, 1906, 211-7. General discussion.

Stock

AUSTEN, F.W. 'Some Christian names from two country parish registers', *E.Rev.* **57**, 1948, 202-4. Stock (formerly Stock Harvard) and Ramsden Bellhouse.

GIBSON, EDWARD PENDARVES. *Registers of Stock Harvard, Co. Essex (from 1563 to 1700).* Mitchell and Hughes, 1881. Includes list of rectors 1334-1700.

GIBSON, E.P. 'The parish registers of Stock Harvard cum Ramsden Bellhouse, Essex', *Archaeological journal* **37**, 1880, 406-16. Includes extracts.

Stratford

WORRALL, E.S. 'Some Essex Catholic registers, IV: Stratford, 1789-99,' *E.Rev.* **12**, 1970, 117-21. Discussion, not transcript.

Theydon Mount

HOWARD, J.J., & BURKE, H. FARNAM, eds. *Theydon Mount: its lords and rectors, with a complete transcript of the parish registers and monumental inscriptions.* Privately printed, [1894] Includes pedigree of Smith, 16-19th c.

G., G. 'Extracts from the parish registers of Theydon Mount, Essex, which begins 1564', *Collectanea topographica et genealogica* **8**, 1843, 406-8.

Thorndon Park

COVERDALE, P.K. 'Notes on the baptismal register of the Catholic chapel of Thorndon Park, nr. Brentwood, Essex', *E.Rec.* **1**, 1959, 37-45.

Thorpe le Soken

WALLER, WILLIAM CHAPMAN, ed. 'The register of the French church at Thorpe-le-Soken in Essex 1684-1726', in LART, CHARLES EDMUND, ed. *Registers of the French churches of Bristol, Stonehouse and Plymouth.* Huguenot Society of London publications **20**. 1912, appendix.

Thurrock

BENTON, A. 'A perfect scramble: Thurrock marriages in London before 1754', *Panorama: journal of the Thurrock Local History Society* **30**, 1989, 23-30.

Toppesfield

BARNES, H.B., & MORANT, PHILIP, eds. *The register of baptisms, marriages and burials at St. Margaret's, Toppesfield parish, Essex Co., England, 1559-1650, and some account of the parish.* Topsfield, Massachussets: Merrill Press, 1905.

Waltham High Cross

WINTERS, W. *Our parish registers, being three hundred years of curious local history, as collected from the original registers, churchwarden's accounts and monumental records of the parish of Waltham Holy Cross.* Waltham Abbey: the author, 1885.

Walthamstow

ROEBUCK, GEORGE EDWARD, ed. *Walthamstow marriages from 24 February 1650 until the date of civil registration 1 July, 1837, abstracted from the parish registers.* Official publication **25**. Walthamstow: Walthamstow Antiquarian Society, 1931.

FORSTER, THOMAS, et al. 'Marriages at Walthamstow 1650-1837', in ROEBUCK, G.E. ed. *E.P.R.M.* **4**; *P.P.R.S.* **214**. 1914, 1-71.

Widford

'Marriage at Widford, 1619 to 1837', in
ARNOLD-WALLINGER, R.N., ed. *E.P.R.M.* **3.**
P.P.R.S. **200.** 1913, 131-96.

Witham

H., A.D. 'Marriages of Suffolk', *E.A.M.* **1933,**
3. At Witham, Essex.

Woodford

An index to burials for Woodford, Essex,
1638-1812. 1 fiche. East of London F.H.S.,
[198-?]

Woodham Walter

BROWNE, ROBERT H. 'Parish registers I:
Woodham Walter', *E.Rev.* **1,** 1892, 97-162.
Extracts only, 1622-1800.

Wormingford

STUART, NEVILLE, ed. 'Marriages at
Wormingford, 1559-1837', in PHILLIMORE,
W.P.W., ed. *E.P.R.M.* **1.** *P.P.R.S.* **101.** 1909,
81-101.

Writtle

'Marriages at Writtle, 1634 to 1837', in
ARNOLD-WALLINGER, R.N., ed. *E.P.R.M.* **3.**
P.P.R.S. **200.** 1913, 77-130.

7. MONUMENTAL INSCRIPTIONS

Monumental inscriptions frequently provide
information additional to that found in
parish registers, and are a valuable source of
genealogical information, especially for
recent centuries. For an extensive study of
Essex inscriptions, including pedigrees, see:
CHANCELLOR, FREDERIC. *The ancient*
 sepulchral monuments of Essex: a record
 of interesting tombs in Essex churches
 and some account of the persons and
 families connected with them.
Chelmsford: Edmund Durrant, 1890.
Extensive; includes pedigrees.
Cemeteries in metropolitan Essex are listed
in:
WOLFSTON, PATRICIA S. *Greater London*
 cemeteries and crematoria. 3rd ed., revised
 by Cliff Webb, Society of Genealogists,
 1994.
There are a number of briefer general works:
K. 'The monumental heraldry of Essex', *East*
 Anglian **1-4,** 1864-71, *passim.*
PROBERT, CHAS K. 'Monumental inscriptions
 and arms in Essex', *East Anglian* **2,** 1866,
 313. Lists parishes covered by a
 transcription made by the author.
'A collection of interesting & curious
 epitaphs (connected with Essex)', *Essex*
 notebook and Suffolk gleaner **6-8** 1885,
 passim.
The collections of antiquaries are described
in two articles:
PROBERT, W.G.C. 'Arms and epitaphs in parish
 churches, chiefly of Suffolk and Essex,
 visited by William Tyllotson between 1594
 and 1600', *Suffolk Institute of*
 Archaeology **19,** 1927, 78-9. Description of
 a 17th c. transcription.
STEER, FRANCIS W. 'The Arkesden heraldic
 manuscript', *E.Rev.* **60,** 1951, 135-42.
 Includes notes on heraldry in various
 churches.
For inscriptions relating to Essex inhabitants
found in Suffolk, see:
PARTRIDGE, CHARLES. 'Essex inscriptions in
 Suffolk churchyards', *E.Rev.* **45,** 1936, 174-
 7 & 239-42; **46,** 1937, 109-12 & 170-72.

Essex brasses have received attention from a number of authors. For a listing of their works, see:
BRIGGS, NANCY. 'A bibliography of Essex brasses', *Transactions of the Monumental Brass Society* **11**, 1971, 149-61.
The standard work on Essex brasses is:
The monumental brasses of Essex. 2 pts. Ashford: Monumental Brass Society, 1948-51.
See also:
CHRISTY, MILLER, PORTEOUS, W.W., & SMITH, BERTRAM. 'The monumental brasses of Essex', in KELWAY, A. CLIFTON. ed. *Memorials of old Essex.* Bemrose & Sons, 1908, 118-57.
CHRISTY, MILLER, & PORTEOUS, W.W. 'On some interesting Essex brasses', *T.E.A.S.* N.S., **6**, 1898, 146-70; **7**, 1900, 1-31, 207-48; **8**, 1903, 15-54 & 249-85; **9**, 1906, 22-67; **10**, 1909, 181-227; **11**, 1911, 101-46 & 321-34; **12**, 1913, 225-53.
CHRISTY, MILLER, & PORTEOUS, W.W. 'On some interesting Essex brasses', *E.Rev.* **7** 1898, 31-50, **9**, 1900, 77-91, **10**, 1901, 84-101.
CHRISTY, MILLER, & PORTEOUS, W.W. 'Some interesting Essex brasses', *Reliquary* N.S., **5**, 1899, 9-21; **7**, 1901, 73-88; **9**, 1903, 145-62; **14**, 1908, 39-46 & 124-37.
CHRISTY, MILLER, PORTEOUS, W. WADE, & SMITH, E. B. 'Some interesting Essex brasses', *Transactions of the Monumental Brass Society* **4**, 1900, 45-60. From various parishes.
CHRISTY, MILLER, & PORTEOUS, W.W. 'Some lost Essex brasses', *Transactions of the Monumental Brass Society* **3**, 1897-9, 254-64.
CHRISTY, MILLER, & PORTEOUS, W.W. 'Some Essex brasses recently refixed', *T.E.A.S.* N.S., **8**, 1903, 363-8.
FRANKS, AUGUSTUS W. '[Monumental brasses of Essex]', *Proceedings of the Society of Antiquaries* 2nd series **7**, 1876-8, 147-54.
For discussions of two collections of brass rubbings, see:
BENTON G. MONTAGU. 'The A.H. Brown collection of brass rubbings', *T.E.A.S.* N.S. **19**, 1930, 321-3. Description of an antiquary's collection.

FREETH, STEPHEN. 'The brass-rubbings in the Society's collections', *E.A.H.* **11**, 1979, 119-233. Includes list of rubbings of 'lost' brasses.
Hatchments are fully listed in:
SUMMERS, PETER, & TITTERTON, JOHN. *Hatchments in Britain 6: Cambridgeshire, Essex, Hertfordshire, Huntingdonshire and Middlesex.* Phillimore & Co., 1985.

B. *By Place*

Arkesden
BUTCHER, CHAS. H. 'Some heraldic glass in North-West Essex', *E.Rev.* **30**, 1921, 193-9. At Arkesden, Lindsell, Little Chesterford, Shalford and Stambourne.

Ashen
CHRISTY, MILLER, & PORTEOUS, W.W. On the brasses in Ashen, Fryerning and Great Leighs churches', *E.Rev.* **3**, 1894, 119-31. See also 200-202.

Aveley
AUSTIN, D.C. 'The church brasses of Aveley and Stifford', *Panorama: the journal of the Thurrock History Society.* **12**, 1968, 18-28.

Barking
CLIFFORD, TONY. 'St. Margarets churchyard, Barking', *C.A.* **63**, 1994, 3-8.

Birdbrook
CHANCELLOR, FRED. 'Essex churches, I: St. Augustines, Birdbrook', *E.Rev.* **1**, 1892, 33-41. Includes lists of monuments, and of rectors and patrons.

Blackmore
CHANCELLOR, FRED. 'Essex churches XXII: St. Laurence, Blackmore', *E.Rev.* **8**, 1899, 65-86. Includes 18 monumental inscriptions, list of armorial inscriptions, list of armorial shields and lists of priors, vicars and curates.

Bobbingworth
CRISP, F.A., ed. *Sepulchral memorials of Bobbingwoth, Essex, with genealogical notes and pedigrees* Frederick Arthur Crisp, 1888. Includes many will abstracts, pedigrees of Bourne and Oliver (folded).

Boreham

CHANCELLOR, FRED. 'Essex churches III: St. Andrews, Boreham', *E.Rev.* **1**, 1892, 150-63. Includes list of 36 monuments, and of vicars.

SMITH, WILLIAM J.T. *Memorials inside and outside the church.* Boreham histories 6. [Chelmsford?]: [W.J.T. Smith], 1983. At Boreham.

Borley

MARY CATHERINE, SISTER. 'Papist tombs in Essex churches IX: Borley and Navestock', *E.Rev.* **5**(2), 1963, 58-66.

Bowers Gifford

Monumental Inscriptions at St. Margaret's Bowers Gifford. E.S.F.H., [199-?] Not seen.

Bulmer

Monumental inscriptions at St. Andrews church, Bulmer, Essex, 1711-1979. 1 fiche [ ]: E.S.F.H., [199-?]

Chelmsford

Monumental inscriptions at London Road non-conformist cemetery, Chelmsford, Essex. 1846-1981. 1 fiche. [ ]: E.S.F.H. [199-?]

Chingford

BONE, K.C. 'Chingford monumental inscriptions', *Chingford notes passim* Brief notes.

'Monumental inscriptions in the churchyard at Chingford, Essex', *Fragmenta Genealogica* **13**, 1909, 65-101.

Coggeshall

DUNKIN, A.J., ed. *Monumenta Anglicana: Coggeshall.* Privately published, 1844. Includes many monumental inscriptions.

Colchester

BENHAM, M. *Among the tombs of Colchester.* Colchester: Benham & Co., 1880. Descriptions of churchyards *etc.,* with many inscriptions.

CHRISTY, MILLER, & SMITH, E. BERTRAM. 'The monumental brasses of Colchester', *T.EA.S.* N.S., **13**, 1915, 38-52.

Cold Norton

See Great Bardfield

Colne Engaine

Monumental inscriptions at St. Andrew, Colne Engaine, Essex, 1745-1977. 1 fiche. [ ]: E.S.F.H., [199-?].

Corringham

See Grays Thurrock

Cressing

Monumental inscriptions at All Saints church and churchyard, Cressing, 1780-1990. 1 fiche [ ]: E.S.F.H., [199-?].

Danbury

COLLINS, ANDREW. *The knights of Danbury.* Wickford: Earthquake Books, 1985. Discussion of the knights whose effigies are in this church — especially St. Clere or Sinclair.

Dovercourt

See Harwich

Downham

MARY CATHERINE, SISTER. 'Papist tombs in Essex churches III: Downham', *E.Rev.* **3**(2), 1961, 83-6.

Fairstead

Monumental inscriptions at St. Mary's, Fairstead. Fiche. E.S.F.H., [199-?] Not seen.

Faulkbourne

'Faulkbourne church', *T.E.A.S.* N.S., **1**, 1878, 232-50. Includes monumental inscriptions and heraldry.

Monumental inscriptions at St. Germanus church, Faulkbourne, near Witham, Essex, 1576-1988. 1 fiche. [ ]: E.S.F.H., [199-].

Felsted

CHANCELLOR, FRED. 'Essex churches XIX: Holy Cross, Felstead', *E.Rev.* **6**, 1897, 25-44. Includes 19 memorial inscriptions, with a list of vicars, and extracts from the parish register concerning the Riche family.

Finchingfield

See Great Bardfield and Pentlow

Forest Gate

REDMAN, MARGARET. 'In memoriam at Forest Gate', *C.A.* **24** 1984, 2-3. Memorial to members of Woodgrange Methodist Church who fell in the 1914-18 War. Includes list.

Frating

Monumental inscriptions in the churchyard at Frating, Essex, 1720-1973. 1 fiche. [ ]: E.S.F.H., [199-?].

Fryerning

See Ashen

Gosfield

WORRALL, EDW. W. 'A funeral monument in Gosfield churchyard', *E.Rev.* **6**(3), 1964, 107-11. Commemorating nuns of the Poor Clares of Gravelines, refugees in the Napoleonic wars.

Grays Thurrock

AUSTIN, H. 'The church brasses of Grays Thurrock, Orsett and Corringham', *Panorama: the journal of the Thurrock History Society* **14**, 1969-70, 65-72.

Great Baddow

CHANCELLOR, FRED. 'Essex churches IX: St. Mary-the-Virgin, Great Baddow', *E.Rev.* **3**, 1894, 92-104. Includes 9 monumental inscriptions, plus a list of vicars.

MARY CATHERINE, SISTER. 'Papist tombs in Essex churches XIV: Great Baddow and Writtle', *E.Rec.* **7**(2) 1965, 72-7.

Great Bardfield

MARY CATHERINE, SISTER. 'Papist tombs in XIII: Great Bardfield, Little Sampford, and Finchingfield', *E.Rev.* **6**(3), 1964, 76-83.

Great Bromley

CHRISTY, MILLER, & PORTEOUS, W.W. 'On some brasses in the churches for Great Bromley, Cold Norton, Shapland, Stebbing, and Wenden Lofts, Essex', *E.Rev.* **6**, 1896, 213-24.

Great Clacton

CHANCELLOR, FRED. 'Essex churches XX: St. John the Baptist, Great Clacton', *E.Rev.* **6** 1887, 193-204. Includes 9 monumental inscriptions.

Great Henny

Monumental inscriptions at St. Mary's, Great Henny. Fiche. E.S.F.H., [199-.] Not seen.

Great Leighs

CLARK, ANDREW. 'Village churchyard monuments 1721-1820', *E.Rev.* **23**, 1914, 185-8. Discussion of those at Great Leighs.

CLARK, A. ' Heraldic glass formerly at Great Leighs', *E. Rev.* **23**, 1914, 44.

See also Ashen

Great Oakley

'Great Oakley, Co. Essex', *Fragmenta Genealogica* **6**, 1901 19-22. Monumental inscriptions.

Great Warley

Monumental inscriptions at the old churchyard, Gt. Warley 1661-1930. 1 fiche. [ ]: E.SF.H., [1992?].

Great Yeldham

E.T. 'Epitaphs and inscriptions in Great Yeldham churchyard, Essex', *E.A.M.*, 1908, 50.

Harlow

BRADFORD, J.G. 'The armorial glass and badges in Harlow church', *T.E.A.S.* **11**, 1911, 347-61.

Harwich

BLOOM, J. HARVEY. *Heraldry and monumental inscriptions in the churches, nonconformist chapels and burial grounds of Harwich, Dovercourt and Ramsey, in the Hundred of Tendring and County of Essex.* Hemsworth: C.E. Turner, 1893. Includes pedigrees of Bridge, Coleman, Cox, Deane and Phillipson, 17-18th c.

Hatfield Broad Oak

GALPIN, F.W. 'Notes on the tombs and memorial tablets of the parish church, Hatfield Broad Oak', *T.E.A.S.* N.S. **4**, 1893, 235-44.

Highwood

Monumental inscriptions at St. Paul's Highwood. Fiche. E.S.F.G., [1996].

Hornchurch
CHANCELLOR, FRED. 'Essex churches XVI: St. Andrews, Hornchurch', *E.Rev.* **5**, 1896, 18-40. Includes 41 monumental inscriptions; also lists of vicars.

Hutton
MARY CATHERINE, ! SISTER. 'Papist tomb in Essex churches XV: Hutton and Witham', *E.Rec.* **7**(3), 1965, 126-31.

Ingatestone
MARY CATHERINE, ! SISTER. 'Papist tombs in Essex churches V: Ingatestone', *E.Rec.* **4**(1), 1962, 31-5. See also **4**(2), 1962, 65-70; **6**(1), 1964, 13-15.

Ingrave
'Papist tombs in Essex churches VI: Ingrave & Thorndon', *E.Rec.* **4**(1), 1962, 36-9.

Kelvedon
HAY, E.F. *Notes on the parish church of St. Mary the Virgin, Kelvedon (Easterford): inscription and other records.* Colchester: Wiles & Son, 1903.

Kelvedon Hatch
MARY CATHERINE, SISTER. 'Papist tombs in Essex churches VIII: Kelvedon Hatch', *E.Rec.* **2**(3), 1960, 127-8, **4**(3), 1962.

Lexden
Monumental inscriptions at St. Leonard'S church & churchyard, Lexden. Essex. Fiche. [ ]: E.S.F.H., [199-?]. Includes Henry Lexden's index of 1883.

Leyton
'[Monumental inscriptions at] Leyton County High School, Essex Road, Leytonstone', *Roots in the Forest: the journal of the Waltham Forest Family History Society* **7**(2), 1995, 26-29. Includes rolls of honour for wars of 1914-18 and 1939-45

Lindsell
See Arkesden

Little Baddow
Monumental Inscriptions of Little Baddow United Reformed Church. Fiche. E.S.F.H., [1995]. Not seen.

Little Braxted
Monumental Inscriptions of St. Nicholas church and churchyard, Little Braxted. Fiche. E.S.F.H., 1991. Not seen.

Little Chesterford
See Lindsell

Little Easton
Parish of Little Easton: churchyard inscriptions (including a plan of the yard). Braintree: Chas. Joscelyne, 1926.

Little Horkesley
MARKHAM, CLEMENTS ROBERT. 'Notes on Little Horkesley church, Essex', *Archaeologia* **46**, 1881, 269-80. Includes notes on monumental inscriptions.

Little Sampford
See Great Bardfield

Mucking
Monumental inscription at St. John the Baptist [Mucking] 1607-1976. 1 fiche. [ ]: E.S.F.H. [199-?]

Navestock
CHANCELLOR, FRED. 'Essex churches XV: St. Thomas the Apostle, Navestock', *E.Rev.* **4**, 1895, 213-34. Includes 42 monumental inscriptions; also list of vicars.
See also Borley.

Newham
PARK, STEPHEN. 'Parishes and cemeteries in Newham', *C.A.* **19** 1983, 17-20. List with map.

Orsett
STUCHFIELD, H.MARTIN. 'The monumental brasses of Essex: Orsett', *E.J.* **27**(1), 1992, 13-16.
Monumental inscriptions at St. Giles and All Saints church, Orsett, Essex. Fiche. [ ]: E.S.F.H. [1992?] Surveyed in 1992.
See also Grays Thurrock

Pentlow
MARY CATHERINE, SISTER. 'Papist tombs in Essex churches XVIII: Pentlow and Finchingfield, 2', *E.Rec.* **10**, 1868, 1-9.

Rainham
Monumental inscriptions in the churchyard of St. Helen and St. Giles Rainham, Essex, recorded on 15 September 1985. 1 fiche [ ]: East of London F.H.S., [199-?] Fiche also includes *Monumental inscriptions in the churchyard of St. Mary and St. Peter, Wennington, Essex, recorded on 14 September 1985.*

Ramsey
See Harwich

Rettendon
CHANCELLOR, FRED. 'Essex churches XI: All Saints, Rettendon', *E.Rev.* 3, 1894, 224-35. Includes monumental inscriptions and a list of rectors.

Rivenhall
Monumental inscriptions at St. Mary and All Saints, Rivenhall, Essex, 1780-1988. 1 fiche. [ ]: E.S.F.H., [199-?].

Romford
BAKER, JEANNE. *Index to St. Edwards Church Romford, Essex, inscriptions in the church and churchyard, copied by Alfred Bennett-Bamford, 1887-97.* 1 fiche. East of London F.H.S., 1992.

Runwell
MARY CATHERINE, SISTER. 'Papist tombs in Essex churches X: Runwell', *E.Rec.* 5(3), 1963, 99-104.

Sandon
CHANCELLOR, FRED. 'Essex churches XVII: St. Andrew's, Sandon', *E.Rev.* 5, 1896, 68-84. Includes monumental inscriptions; also lists of rectors.

Shalford
See Lindsell

Shopland
See Great Bromley

South Ockendon
AUSTIN, HAZEL. 'The church brasses of South Ockendon and West Thurrock', *Panorama: the journal of the Thurrock Local History Society* 13, 1970, 53-60.

South Weald
MARY CATHERINE, SISTER. 'Papist tombs in Essex churches XII: South Weald', *E.Rev.* 6(2), 1964, 65-74.
'Monuments in Weald church in Essex', *Fragmenta Genealogica* 9, 1903, 79-85.

Springfield
CHANCELLOR, FRED. 'Essex churches VIII: All Saints, Springfield', *E.Rev* 3, 1894, 50-63. Includes 17 monumental inscriptions, and a list of rectors.

Stambourne
See Lindsell

Stanford Rivers
MARY CATHERINE, SISTER. 'Papist tombs in Essex churches, IV: Stanford Rivers', *E.Rec.* 3(3) 1961, 137-43.

Stanway
S[TEINMAN], G.S. 'Epitaphs and extracts from the register at Stanway church, Essex', *Collectanea topographica et genealogica* 4, 1837, 305-8.

Stebbing
See Great Bromley

Stifford
See Aveley

Terling
Monumental inscriptions at All Saints Church & cemetery, United Reformed Church, Terling, Essex, 1558-1990. Fiche. [ ]: E.S.F.H., [1991?]

Theydon Garnon
Monumental inscriptions in All Saints churchyard, Theydon Garnon. Fiche E.S.F.H., [199-?] Not seen.

Thorndon
See Ingrave

Thurrock
HARROLD, CHRISTOPHER. 'The Thurrock hatchments', *Panorama: the journal of the Thurrock History Society* 17, 1973-4, 44-51; 18, 1974-5, 60.

Tillingham

BAXTER, JACK H., ed. *Monumental inscriptions in the Baptist burial ground, Tillingham, Essex.* [ ]: E.S.F.H., [199-?].

CHANCELLOR, FRED. 'Essex churches VI: St. Nicholas, Tillingham', *E.Rev.* **2**, 1893, 146-59. See also **3**, 1894, 75; **5**, 1896, 231.

Tolleshunt Knights

Monumental inscriptions at All Saints churchyard (a) and new burial ground (b) at Tolleshunt Knights. 1 fiche. [ ]: E.S.F.H., [199-?]

Upminster

BENTON, TONY. 'Upminster: anatomy of a war memorial', *C.A.,* **53**, 1993, 3-8. Includes names, 1914-18.

Wakes Colne

Monumental inscriptions in the church Wakes Colne, Essex. 1 fiche. [ ]: E.S.F.H., [199-] Filmed from a handwritten trascript.

Walthamstow

CROUCH, C.H. *St. Mary the Virgin, Walthamstow: inscriptions in the church and churchyard. Part I: churchyard memorials (section A).* Walthamstow Antiquarian Society official publications **23**. 1930. Includes pedigrees of Laxham, 18th c.

BARNS, STEPHEN, J. *St. Mary the Virgin, Walthamstow: inscriptions in the church and churchyard, part II. Memorials in the church.* Walthamstow Antiquarian Society official publications **27**. 1932.

HANSON, S., LAW, A.D., & TONKIN, W.G.S. *Marsh Street congregations: the Congregational churches and burial ground in Marsh Street, Walthamstow.* Walthamstow Antiqurian Society, 1969 occasional publication **11**, 1969. Primarily monumental inscriptions; also include list of ministers.

Wendon Lofts
See Great Bromley

Wennington
See Rainham

West Thurrock
See South Ockendon

Witham

Monumental inscriptions at St. Nicholas parish church, Witham, Essex, 1584-1988. 1 fiche. [ ]: E.S.F.H., [199-?]

Witham. Howbridge Hall

PARTRIDGE, CHARLES. 'Heraldry at Howbridge Hall, Witham', *E.Rev.* **46**, 1937, 198-204; **47**, 1938, 32-5. Includes pedigree of Fitzherbert, 15-16th c.

Woodford

LITTEN, JULIAN W.S. 'Landscaping a churchyard', *Genealogists magazine* **17**, 1974, 484-5. How it was done at St. Mary's, Woodford.

Woodham Walter

CHANCELLOR, FRED. 'Essex churches II: St. Michaels, Woodham Walter', *E.Rev.* **1**, 1892, 87-96. Includes list of monuments, and of rectors and patrons, with extracts from the parish register.

Writtle

MARY CATHERINE, SISTER. 'Papist tombs in Essex churches II: Writtle'. *E.Rec.* **3**(1), 1961, 31-7. Of Weston, Pinchon and Petre families.
See also Great Baddon

C.By Surname

Barfoot

C[ARTER], H.M. 'Brass of Robert Barfoot at Lambourne: palimpsests found', *T.E.A.S.* N.S. **1**(3), 1964, 215-6.

NORRIS, LAURIE, & NORRIS, MALCOLM. 'A palimpsest at Lambourne', *Transactions of the Monumental Brass Society* **12**, 1979, 229-38. Brass of Robert Barfoot, 1546.

Barnes

DOW, L. 'Barnes of Malgraves', *T.E.A.S.* N.S. **24**, 1951, 159-60. Brass memorial, 1571.

Beaucock

ELLIOT, H.L. 'The memorial stone of a forgotten Essex worthy', *T.E.A.S.* **10**, 1909, 43-6. Edward Beaucock, 1665.

Boothby
See Heathcote

Borrell
'Brass of John Borrell (1531)', *E.Rev.* **1**, 1892, 231-5.

Bourchier

BAYLEY, T.D.S. 'The Bourchier shield in Halstead church', *T.E.A.S.* N.S., **25**(1), 1955, 80-100.

Braybrooke

O'LEARY, J.G. 'Two monuments', *Saffron Walden history* **17**, 1980, 23. Braybrooke family inscriptions, 19-20th c.

Browne

GRIMES, R., & GRIMES, H. 'A palimpsest shield at Stow Maries', *Transactions of the Monumental Brass Society* **12**, 1979, 271-7. Shield of Mary Browne nee Cammocke of Maldon, died 1602. Includes pedigrees of Boteler of Eastry and Browne of Flamberds.

Chapman

RENDALL, GERALD H. 'Dedham tombstones', *T.E.A.S.* N.S., **18**, 1928, 245-53. Tombs of Edmund Chapman, 1602, and John Rogers, 1636.

Coke

BENTON, G. MONTAGUE. 'The Coke and Wilde brass, 1606, at Great Totham, *T.E.A.S.* N.S., **23**, 1945-7, 141-4.

Curgenven

See Lean

Darcy

BRIGGS, NANCY. 'The brasses of the Darcy family at Tolleshunt D'Arcy, Essex', *Transactions of the Monumental Brass Society* **9**(7), 1960, 338-53. Includes pedigree, 15-17th c.

De la Pole

MANNING, C.J. 'Notice of an undescribed sepulchral brass', *Archaeological journal* **4**, 1847, 338-40. At Saffron Walden; memorial of John and Joan De La Pole, 15th c. Includes pedigree.

De Vere

FAIRWEATHER, F.H. 'Calne Priory, Essex and the burials of the Earls of Oxford', *Archaeologia* **87**, 1935, 275-95, De Vere family monuments medieval.

POWELL, J. ENOCH. 'The riddles of Bures', *E.A.H.* **6**, 1974, 90-98. Monuments of the De Vere family, medieval.

PROBERT, GEOFFREY. 'The riddles of Bures unravelled', *E.A.H.* **16**, 1984-5, 53-64. De Vere family monument, reply to Powell.

Dunstanville

See Rhodes

Fitzralph

BURNETT, MONTGOMERY. 'The Fitzralph brass at Pebmarsh', *E.A.H.* 1974, 99-101. Medieval; includes pedigree.

PIGGOT, JOHN. 'Notes on the brass of Sir William Fitz-Ralph, c.1323 in Pebmarsh church, Essex', *Reliquary* **9**, 1868-9, 193-200.

PIGGOT, JOHN. 'On the brass of Sir William Fitz Ralph, c. 1323, in Pebmarsh, Essex', *T.E.A.S.* **4**, 1869, 132-6.

Gayselee

LEWIS, R.R., & COCKELL, D.J. 'Discovery of brass to Walter Gayselee, c. 1370, at Ingrave', *T.E.A.S.* **23**, 1945-7, 169-70. See also 351.

Gernon

HOPE, W.H. ST. J. 'Notes on an early enamelled shield of the arms of Gernon, found at Leez Priory, Essex', *Proceedings of the Society of Antiquaries* 2nd series **22**, 1907-9, 117-19.

Giffard

KING, H.W. 'On a recently discovered monumental brass belonging to Bowers Gifford church', *T.E.A.S* **1**, 1858, 93-8. Sir John Giffard, 1348.

Hallet

MARSHALL, GEORGE W. 'Hallet arms in Little Dunmow church', *East Anglian* **3**, 1869, 309-10. See also **4** 1871, 81.

Harvey

HARVEY, W.J. 'Harvey: coffin inscriptions in Harvey vault, Hempstead church, Co. Essex', *M.G.H.* 2nd series **1**, 1886, 357-62.

'Harvey: monumental inscriptions, Hempstead church, G. Essex, in Harvey Chapel', *M.G.H.* 2nd series **1**, 1886, 384-8. Includes extracts from the parish register, 17-19th c.

Inscriptions in Harvey vault and chapel, Hempstead church, Co. Essex, and extracts from the parish register of Hempstead, with notes. Mitchell and Hughes, 1886.

Heathcote
BONE, K.C. 'Chingford monumental inscriptions, I: monument: a short description', *Chingford notes* 1(3), 1975, 15-16.

Hills
SIER, L.C. 'Monument at Colne Park', *E.Rev.* **46**, 1937, 185-8. Hills family monument, 18-19th c.

Honywood
BENHAM, W. GURNEY. 'Honywood memorials and the famous Honywood cup', *E.Rev.* **42**, 1934, 109-13.

Howard
'Coffin-plate inscriptions in the Howard vault, Saffron Walden church', *M.G.H.* 2nd series **5**, 1894, 127-8. 18th c.

Hubbarde
BENTON, G. MONTAGU. 'Brass to John Hubbarde, 1537, at Great Bromley', *T.E.A.S.* N.S., **21**, 1937, 334. Includes will.

Kendale
See Smith

Larder
GILBERT, WILLIAM. 'The brass to Walter Larder, in the parish church of St. Andrew, North Weald Basset, Essex', *T.E.A.S.* N.S., **11**, 1911, 30-35. Includes will, 1531, and extracts from the parish register, 1579-1616.

Lean
KENT, ALAN. 'Memorial to Peter Curgenven, 1684-1729, Great Waltham parish church, Essex', *Cornwall Family History Society journal* **51**, 1989, 25. The deceased was actually a member of the Lean family of Lelant, Cornwall.

Leigh
BROWN, RICHARD. 'The Leigh memorials in Chingford old church; their history and conservation', *Roots in the Forest: the journal of the Waltham Forest Family History Society* 4(2), 1986, 24-6. Includes pedigree, 17th c.

Maltoun
See Waltham

Mordaunt
CHRISTY, MILLER, & PORTEOUS, W.W. 'An Essex brass', *T.E.A.S.* N.S., **16**, 1923, 205-9. Of William Mordaunt, 1518, at Hempstead.

Parker
BRIGGS, NANCY. 'The Parker brass at Brentwood, Essex', *Transactions of the Monumental Brass Society* **10**, 1966, 154-5.

Partridge
P.R. 'Partridge of Lexden Hundred, Co. Essex: monumental inscriptions', *East Anglian* N.S. **7**, 1897-8, 105-6.

Petre
'Inscriptions on the Petre monuments in Ingatestone church', *Ingatestone and Fryerning Historical and Archeaological Society bulletin* **17**, 1979, 8-12.

Rampstone
HARRISON, GEO. H. ROGERS. 'Notes on a monumental brass effigy in Great Parndon church', *T.E.A.S.* **3**, 1865, 204-5. Effigy of Rowland Rampston, 1598.

Rhodes
GOODALL, JOHN A. 'A lost brass from Walden Abbey, Essex', *Coat of arms* N.S., 9(156), 1991, 160-61. Rhodes and Dunstanville families, medieval.

Rich
ESDAILE, ARUNDELL. 'The monument of the first Lord Rich at Felsted', *T.E.A.S.* N.S., **22**, 1940, 59-67. 1581.

Rochester
BRIGGS, N. 'The Rochester brasses in the south aisle of Terling church, Essex', *Transactions of the Monumental Brass Society* **9**, 1961, 429-38. Includes pedigrees, 16th c.

Rogers
See Chapman

Smith
'Inscriptions on columns in Rayleigh church', *T.E.A.S.* N.S., **22**, 1940, 142-3. Relating to Roger Smith and Henry Kendale, 15th c.

Stanley

L., F. DE. 'A Stanley monument', *Cheshire sheaf* 3rd series, **14**, 1919, 62-3. 16th c., Walthamstow.

Strype

BREN, R. 'Strype memorial slab in Leyton parish church', *E.Rev.*, **41**, 1932, 193-7. 1732.

Tanfield

STEER, FRANCIS W. 'The Tanfield monument at Margaretting', *E.Rev.* **53**, 1944, 105-9. Medieval-17th c.

Tedcastell

CROUCH, WALTER. 'The Tedcastell brass at Barking', *E.Rev.* **2**, 1893, 246-8. Brass to John Tedcastell, 1611/12.

Waldegrave

ELLIOT, HENRY L. 'Waldegrave inscriptions at Borley, Essex', *East Anglian* N.S. **8**, 1899-1900, 145. Sir Edmund Waldegrave, 16th c.

Waltham

CHRISTY, MILLER & PORTEOUS, W.W. 'The monumental brasses at Little Waltham church, Essex', *E.Rev.* **2**, 1893, 45-8. Commemorating Richard Waltham, 1426, and John Maltoun, 1447.

Wilde

See Coke

Williamson

WILLIAMS, J.F. 'Monumental brasses discovered at Chelmsford Cathedral', *T.E.A.S.* N.S., **21**, 1937, 134-5. Williamson family, early 17th c.

Woodthorpe

BENTON, G. MONTAGU. 'Brass of Ayres Woodthorpe, St. Peter's church, Colchester', *T.E.A.S.* N.S. **13**, 1915, 309-11. 1534.

8. PROBATE RECORDS

A General

Probate records – wills, inventories, administration bonds, *etc.*, constitute an invaluable source of genealogical information. It is usually the case that wills identify all surviving children. Many Essex wills were proved in the Prerogative Court of Canterbury. There are a variety of indexes and abstracts of these wills, which are listed in Stuart Raymond's *English genealogy: a bibliography.* All Prerogative Court wills for Essex, 1558-1603 are fully abstracted in:

EMMISON, F. G. *Elizabethan life: wills of Essex gentry & merchants, proved in the Prerogative Court of Canterbury.* Essex Record Office publication **71**. 1978.

Essex wills were also proved in a variety of other courts. An extensive index to wills at Chelmsford is available; it lists wills of the Archdeaconry of Essex from 1400, the Archdeaconry of Colchester from 1500, the Archdeaconry of Middlesex (Essex and Hertfordshire jurisdictions) from 1441, the peculiar of Writtle with Roxwell from 1607, the peculiar of Good Easter from 1613, the peculiar of Bocking Deanery from 1665 and the peculiar of the Liberty of the Sokens from 1632. See:

EMMISON, F.G., ed. *Wills at Chelmsford (Essex and East Hertfordshire).* 3 vols. Index Library **78-9, 84**. British Record Society, 1958-69. Contents: v.1. 1400-1619. v.2. 1620-1720. v.3. 1721-1858.

Many wills from Chingford, Epping, Leyton, Loughton, Nazeing, Waltham Holy Cross, Walthamstow, Woodford and other Essex parishes were proved in the Commissary Court of London, and are indexed in:

FITCH, MARC, ed. *Index to testamentary records in the Commissary Court of London (London Division) now preserved in Guildhall Library.* Index Library **82, 86 & 97**. British Record Society, 1969-85. Contents: v.1. 1374-1488. v.2 1489-1570. v.3. 1571-1625.

Most Essex wills for the Elizabethan period, 1558-1603, are now in print, thanks to a major project conducted by F.G. Emmison, the former county archivist. For an introductory lecture on this project, see:

EMMISON, F.G. *Treasures of social history:* *Essex wills: an introduction to the Elizabethan Essex wills series.* [ ]: Friends of Historic Essex, 1990.
See also:
EMMISON, F.G. 'Elizabethan Essex wills', *Family history,* **15**(128); N.S., **104**, 1991, 359-69.
EMMISON, F.G. 'Fifty thousand ghosts return: Essex wills 1400-1858', *E.Rev.* **65**, 1956, 27-36. General discussion; includes will of Thomas Knapping of Thaxted, 1626.
EMMISON, F.G. 'A new scheme for printing Essex wills', *Archives* **18**(80), 1988, 214-5. Brief note on the *Essex wills* project.
NEALE, KENNETH. 'Elizabethan wills', *Genealogists magazine* **24**(8), 1993 354-55. Discussion of Emmison's work.
For the actual wills, see:
EMMISON, F.G., ed. *Essex wills (England) vol.1: 1558-1565.* Washington: National Geographical Society, 1982.
EMMISON, F.G., ed. *Essex wills (England) vol. 2: 1565-1571. Archdeaconry of Colchester, Archdeaconry of Middlesex (Essex Division) (preserved in the Essex Record Office, Chelmsford).* Boston: New England Historic Genealogical Society, 1983.
EMMISON, F.G., ed. *Essex wills (England) vol. 3: 1571-1577. Archdeaconry of Essex, Archdeaconry of Colchester, Archdeaconry of Middlesex (Essex Division) (Preserved in the Essex Record Office, Chelmsford).* Boston: New England Historic Genealogical Society, 1986.
EMMISON, F.G. ed. *Essex wills: the Archdeaconry courts 1577-1584. E.R.O. publications* **96**. Colchester: Essex Record Office, 1987. Further vols. cover 1583-1592, (1989; publication **101**); 1591-1597, (1991; publication **114**); and 1597-1603, (1990; publication **107**).
EMMISON, F.G. ed. *Essex wills: the Bishop of London's Commissary Court 1558-1569.* Chelmsford: Essex Record Office / Friends of Historic Essex, 1995.
EMMISON, F.G. ed. *Essex wills, the Bishop of London's Commissary Court 1569-1578.* E.R.O. publications **127**. 1994.
EMMISON, F.G. ed. *Essex wills, the Bishop of London's Commissary Court, 1578-1588.* E.R.O. publication **129**. 1995.

EMMISON, F.G. *Elizabethan life: wills of Essex gentry and yeomen, preserved in the Essex Record Office.* Essex Record Office, publication **75**. 1980.
EMMISON, F.G. *Elizabethan wills of South-West Essex.* Waddesdon: Kylin Press, 1983. Wills proved in the Commissary Court of the Bishop of London.
For other Essex will abstracts, indexes *etc.,* see:
BAMFORD, E. BENNETT. 'Bequests relating to Essex extracted from Calendar of wills proved and enrolled in the Court of Hustings, London', *T.E.A.S.* N.S. **13**, 1915, 253-66. 13-16th c. **14**, 1918, 26-48.
BROUGHTON, THOR.A. 'Essex wills beneficiaries index', *E.F.H.* **39**, 1986, 16-17. Description of a useful index. See also regular updates in *E.F.H.*.
BROUGHTON, THOR.A. 'Indexers and their indexes: the Essex wills beneficiaries index', *Family tree magazine* **10**(2), 1993, 15-16.
BENTON, G. MONTAGU. 'Essex wills at Canterbury', *T.E.A.S.* N.S. **21**, 1934, 234-69. Abstracts of wills proved before the Commissary of the Prior and Chapter of Christ Church, *sede vacante* i.e. whilst the Archbishopric was vacant.
GILBERT, WILLIAM. ed. 'A digest of Essex wills, with particular reference to names of importance in the American colonies', *New York genealogical and biographical record* **40**, 1909, 4-9, 108-14, 155-9 & 276-80; **41**, 1910, 56-60, 175-81 & 367-72; **42**, 1911, 50-57, 193-201 & 319-21. Reprinted in
HOFF, HENRY B., ed. *English origins of American colonists, from the New York genealogical and biographical record.* Baltimore: Genealogical Publishing, 1991, 193-256.
KING, H.W. 'Notices of some ancient wills of inhabitants of the county of Essex', *T.E.A.S.* **1**, 1858, 149-60; **3**, 1863, 53-63, 75-94 & 67-97; **4**, 1869, 1-24, 62, & 147-83, **5**, 1873, 281-93.
KING, H.W. 'Excerpts from ancient wills', *T.E.A.S.* N.S., **1**, 1878, 165-78; **2**, 1884, 55-70 & 359-79; **3**, 1889, 230-237 & 287-303.
MALDEN, H.C. 'Ancient wills', *T.E.A.S.* **5-7**, 1895-1900, *passim*.
'Abstracts of wills of Essex Catholic interest', *E.Rec.* **15**, 1973, 24-5; **16**, 1974, 103-6; **17**, 1975, 52-7 & 91-4; **18**, 1976, 37-40 89-97.

41

B. Local Collections

A number of collections, *etc.*, of will abstracts relating to particular places are available; these are listed here.

Chigwell

O'LEARY, JOHN GERARD. 'Chigwell wills in the fifteenth and sixteenth centuries', *Chigwell Local History Society transactions* **2**, 1974, 17-21. Discussion, not transcripts.

WALLER, WILLIAM CHAPMAN. 'Old Chigwell wills', *T.E.A.S.* N.S. **10**, 1909, 237-45 & 312-9; **11**, 1911, 10-18, 150-9 & 335-46. 14-17th c.

Fingringhoe

BENTON, G. MONTAGU. 'Fingringhoe wills A.D. 1400 to A.D. 1550', *T.E.A.S.* N.S., **20**, 1933, 51-72. Abstracts.

Foulness

EMMISON, F.G., & HALL, OLWEN. 'Life and death in Foulness 1503-1632', *E.J.* **10**(1-2), 2-32. Primarily abstracts of 48 wills.

Great Bromley

BENTON G. MONTAGU. 'Great Bromley wills', *T.E.A.S.* N.S., **23**, 1945-7, 170-73. Abstracts, early 16th c.

Layer de la Haye

'Layer-de-la-Haye wills', *T.E.A.S.* N.S., **21**, 1937, 335-7. Brief abstracts, early 16th c.

Ramsden Bellhouse

See Stock

Roxwell

See Writtle

Stock

AUSTIN, F.W. 'Some Essex wills', *E.Rev.* **56**, 1947, 196-203. Brief extracts from wills of Stock and Ramsden Bellhouse.

Walthamstow

FRY, GEORGE S. *Abstracts of wills relating to Walthamstow, Co. Essex (1335-1559).* Official publications **9**. Walthamstow: Walthamstow Antiquarian Society, 1921.

Weeley

BENTON, G. MONTAGU. 'Weeley church: abstracts from wills, 1510 to 1550', *T.E.A.S.* **21**, 1937, 131-4.

Writtle

STEER, FRANCIS W., ed. *Farm and cottage inventories of mid-Essex, 1635-1749.* 2nd ed. Chichester: Phillimore & Co., 1969. Probate inventories from the peculiar of Writtle (which included the chapelry of Roxwell).

C. Individual

Adly

WILSON, THOS. L. 'Domestic economy at Upminster three centuries ago', *E.Rev.* **15**, 1906, 67-9. Probate inventory of Elizabeth Adly, 1926.

Arnold

'Domestic inventory', *T.E.A.S.* **10**, 1909, 58-9. Probate inventory of John Arnold gent., of Great Warley, 1719.

Barrington

LOWNDES, G. ALAN. 'An inventory of the household goods of Sir Thomas Barrington Bart., at Hatfield Priory, in 1626', *T.E.A.S.* N.S., **3**, 1889, 155-76.

Blyth

'Will of Mary Blyth of Langham, Essex', *E.A.M.* 1907, 113-4.

Bourchier

See Marney

Braybrooke

BRABROOK, EDWARD W. 'The will of Sir Gerard de Braybroke, of Danbury, knt., A.D. 1429', *T.E.A.S.* **5**, 1869, 297-309. Includes folded pedigree, medieval.

Brown

DUNLOP, J. RENTON. 'Genealogical notes', *M.G.H.* 5th series **4**, 1920-22, 242-6. Includes will of Anthony Brown of Southwold, 1565.

Browne

SEARLE, ARTHUR. 'An inventory for Navestock, 1601, *E.J.* **4**(1) 1969, 31-3. Probate inventory of Harry Browne.

Cartwright

SAGE, EDWARD J. 'Essex wills no. 4: Thomas Cartwright, D.D., Bishop of Chester and Vicar of Barking', *East Anglian* **1**, 1864, 388-94. 1689.

Cleveland

SELLERS, ELIZABETH. 'A superabundance of strays: is this a record?', *E.F.H.* **13**, 1979, 10-11. Extracts from the will of Thomas Cleveland of Shalford, 1608.

Coker

WILLIAMS, J.F. 'A rhyming will of 1563', *T.E.A.S.* N.S., **22**, 1940, 139-41. Will of Roger Coker, rector of East Donyland and Hazeleigh.

Convers

LEA, J. HENRY. 'Genealogical gleanings among the English archives', *New England historical and genealogical register* **59**, 1905, 172-7. Convers family wills, 15-17th c.

Cooke

'Essex wills, no. 1', *East Anglian* **1**, 1864, 325-7. Will of Sir Anthony Cooke, 1576.

Copto

REANEY, P.H. 'Copto family of High Easter', *T.E.A.S.* N.S. **25**(1), 1955, 112-4. Will of John Copto, 1470.

Crush

NORRIS, E.G. 'A seventeenth century inventory', *E.Rev.* **15**, 1906, 169-75. Probate inventory of Thomas Crush of Roxwell, 1686.

De Vere

HOPE, WILLIAM H. ST. J., SIR. 'The last testament and inventory of John de Veer, thirteenth Earl of Oxford', *Archaeologia* **66**, 1914-15, 275-348.

ROUND, J.H. 'Two great Vere documents', *T.E.A.S.* N.S. **14**, 1918, 298-302. Discussion of the wills and inventories of John De Vere, Earl of Oxford.

LEWER, H.W. 'The testament and last will of Elizabeth, widow of John de Veer, thirteenth Earl of Oxford', *T.E.A.S.* N.S., **20**, 1933, 7-16. 1537.

Edwards

BROWNE, R.H. 'Inventories of goods', *E.Rev.* **16**, 1907, 204-7. Probate inventories of Thos. Edwards, 1617 (no place given) and William Toller of Ardley, 1620.

Ennows

EDDY, M.R., & RYAN, P.M. 'John Ennows: a previously unknown clay-pipe maker of All Saints, Colchester', *E.A.H.* **15**, 1983, 106-12. Includes probate inventory, 1684.

Fanshawe.

SAGE, EDWARD J. 'Fanshawe wills', *M.G.H.* **2**, 1876, 280-303 & 338-58. Of London, Hertfordshire and Essex, *etc.*, 16-18th c.

'Essex wills, no 5: Sir Richard Fanshawe and Anne, Lady Fanshawe', *East Anglian* **2** 1866, 119-25. 17th c., includes funeral certificate.

Fyrmyn

S., F.H. 'Will of Robert Fyrmyn of Borley, Essex', *E.A.M.* 1917, 52-3 & 55.

Gerard

SAGE, E.J. 'Abstract of the will of Isabelle Gerard of Romford', *M.G.H.* N.S., **1**, 1874, 13. 1637.

Gosnold

LEA, J. HENRY. 'Genealogical gleanings among the English archives', *New England historical and genealogical register* **56**, 1902, 402-7; **57**, 1903, 93-100 & 216-20; **58**, 1905, 311-14 & 396-400; **59**, 1906, 101-3. Gosnold family wills 16-17th c. with some parish register extracts.

Gray

STAHLSCHMIDT, J.C.L. 'The will of Miles Gray, of Colchester, bell founder', *T.E.A.S.* N.S., **3**, 1889, 74-5. 1686.

Harsnett

MUSKETT, J.J. 'Archbishop Harsnett and his will', *East Anglian* N.S., **12**, 1907-8 293-6. An Essex Archbishop of York. Will dated 1631.

Haynes

HAINES, A.M. 'Material relating to the Essex family of Haynes', *New England historical and genealogical register* **49**, 1895, 304-10. Primarily will abstracts, late 17th c., also includes monumental inscriptions.

Heird

WILLIAMS, J.F 'Bequests to Theydon Mount church in 1487', *T.E.A.S.* **19**, 1930, 3316. Notes on the will of John Heird of Hackney, Middlesex, relating to Essex.

Hervey

SPAUL, J.E.H. 'The settlement of Sir George Hervey's estate, 1605-10', *Romford record* **6**, 1974, 21-39. Includes will and various other probate documents.

Houghton
A., F.S. 'Will of Thomas Houghton, clerk, 1549/50', *Cheshire sheaf* 3rd series **19**, 1924, 17-18. Of High Ongar.

Joslin / Josselyn
'Joslin family', *Fragmenta genealogica* **4**, 1899, 1-16. **7**, 1902, 117-9. Wills and administrations, 16-18th c.
FRENCH, ELIZABETH. 'Genealogical research in England: Josselyn', *New England historical and genealogical register* **71**, 1917, 19-33. Josselyn family wills 16-17th c., also includes extracts from various parish registers.

Larder
'Larder and Nicholls wills', *M.G.H.* 2nd series **3**, 1890, 245-6. 16-17th c.

Lovell
'Will of Henry Lovell, Lord Morley', *M.G.H.* **1**, 1868, 61. Of Norfolk, Essex and Hertfordshire, 1489.

Malb
See Marney

Marney
KING, H.W. 'Ancient wills, (No. 9)', *T.E.A.S.* N.S., **1**, 1878, 142-52. Wills of Briget, Lady Marney, of Little Horkesley, 1495, Dame Elizabeth Bourchier, 1499, and William Malb, of Beeleigh Abbey, 1504-5.

Merell
'Two early sixteenth-century wills: Merell of Earls Colne and Coggeshall, Essex', *East Anglian* N.S. **3** 1889-90, 19-22.

Monteny
STEER, F.W. 'Smaller houses and their furnishing in the seventeenth and eighteenth centuries', *Journal of the British Archaeological Association* 3rd series **20-21**, 1958, 140-60. Includes probate inventory of Arnald Monteny of Mountnessing, 1386.

More
BENTON, G. MONTAGU. 'Will of William More, Bishop of Colchester, 1540', *T.E.A.S.* N.S., **23**, 1945-7, 354-6.
DAVIDSON, ALAN. 'A note on the More family', *E.Rec.* **11**, 1970, 12. Note on the will of Cresacre More 1614.

Morley
'The will of John Morley', *E.Rev.*, **11**, 1902, 240-43. Of Halstead, 1777.
See also Lovell

Morse
SOMERSET, HORATIO G. 'Will of Rev. Thomas Morse of Foxearth, County of Essex, England, 1596', *New England historical and genealogical register* **19**, 1865, 264-6.

Nicholls
See Lander

Pelham
'Will of Herbert Pelham, esq., 1672', *New England historical and genealogical register* **18**, 1864, 172-5.

Petre
HOLT, T.G. 'Two eighteenth century Essex wills', *E.Rec.* **12**, 1974, 32-8. Wills of William Petre, 1728, and John Wright of Kelvedon Hall, 1731.

Piryton
GRANT, ERNEST H. 'A Soken will', *T.E.A.S.* N.S., **15**, 1921, 95-7. Will of Richard de Piryton, 1387.

Playter
WADLEY, THOMAS P. 'The Playter family', *Genealogist* N.S., **3**, 1886, 117-8. Will of Anne Playter of Heydon, 1642.

Powlett
EMMISON, F.G. 'Abstract of the will of Frances Powlett, widow', *E.Rec,* **17**, 1975, 13-17. Of Borley, 1599.

Rainsford
RAINSFORD, ALFRED. 'Abstracts from Rainsford wills, inventories, and inquisitions post mortem', *Notes and queries* **158**, 1930, 399-403, 417-9 & 435-8. Of Essex, Oxfordshire, *etc.*

Rebow
RICKWORD, GEORGE. 'An early Georgian inventory', *T.E.A.S.* N.S., **14**, 1918, 16-25. Of Isaac Lemyng Rebow, of Colchester, 1735.

Riche
BROWN, J.R. 'Will of Sir Nathaniel Riche, 1635', *M.G.H.* 3rd series **5**, 1904, 61-3.
'The Rogers family', *New England historical and genealogical register* **17**, 1863, 326-30. Wills of Richard Rogers of Wetherfield, 1618 and John Rogers of Dedham, 1636.

Ryves
'Essex wills, no. 3: Charles Ryves, D.D., of Hornchurch', *East Anglian* 1, 1864, 359.

Sayer
MOSS, REG, & MOSS, LILIAN. 'Benjamin Sayer: testator', *E.F.H.* **68**, 1993, 10-12. Of Coggeshall; notes from his will, 1810.

Semar
'Copy of Katherine Semar's will', *Saffron Walden history* **27**, 1985, 75. 1510.

Sewell
FRENCH, ELIZABETH. 'Genealogical research in England: Sewell', *New England historical and genealogical register* **67**, 1913, 262-70. Sewell family wills, extracts from parish register, etc., 16-17th c. Of Halstead.

Soones
HALL, OLWEN. 'A Dutch weavers house in 1609', *E.J.* 4(2), 1969, 107-9. Probate inventory of John Soones.

Sorrell
CLARK, ANDREW. 'Life of an Essex yeoman, 1672', *E.Rev.* **20**, 1911, 194-7. Probate inventory of James Sorrell of Little Waltham.

Stephenson
A., F.S. 'Wills of Reynold Stephenson of Hornedon on the Hill, 1493', *Cheshire sheaf* **18**, 1923, 4.

Sysley
'Essex wills, no. 2: Clement Synsley of Eastbury Hall, 1578', *East Anglian* 1, 1864, 348-51.

Toller
See Edwards

Waldegrave
'Waldegrave wills', *East Anglian* N.S. 7, 1897-8, 305-7, 322-5, 344-7.

Wanton
KING, H.W. 'A short chapter in the history of the descent of the manor of Horham', *T.E.A.S.* N.S., 3, 1889, 280-4. Will of Sir William Wanton, 1392.

Warner
CLARK, ANDREW. 'An Essex dairy farm, 1629', *E.Rev.* **21**, 1912, 156-9. Probate inventory of William Warner of Hutton.

Wellesley
CAUNT, GEORGE. 'The Wellesleys in Essex', *E.J.* 5(1), 1970, 32-8. 17-19th c.

Whitbred
NOLAN, M.M. 'Two Whitbred wills', *E.Rec.* 7(3), 1965, 115-25. Wills of William Whitbred of Writtle, 1661 and Thomas Whitbred of Great Baddow, 1684.

White
HARTHARN, M.J. 'The will of George White of Hutton', *E.Rec.* **10**, 1968, 100-101. 1584.

Wilford
NOLAN, M.M. 'The will of Ann Wilford of Quendon, 1631', *E.Rec.* **9**, 1967, 86-7.

Wright
See Petre

D. Inquisitions Post Mortem
Prior to the Civil War *inquisitions post mortem* were taken on the deaths of tenants in chief. These list all the lands held, and name the heir. Extensive transcripts and indexes are available at the national level, and are listed in Stuart Raymond's *English genealogy: a bibliography.* For Essex, three *inquisitions* have been separately published:

Burford
STAHLSCHMIDT, J.C.L. 'Robert Burford of London, bellfounder', *T.E.A.S.* N.S., 3, 1889, 138-40. *Inquisition post mortem,* listing his Essex property, 1418.

Crowley
'Inquisition post mortem of Thomas Crowley, sen.', *E.Rec.* **8**, 1966, 113-8. Translation; taken in 1560.

Wiseman
SKEET, FRANCIS, J.A. 'Thomas Wiseman of Wimbish: his *inquisitio post mortem* 28 Eliz. (1586), with some notes of his family', in *Miscellanea* 7. Publications of the Catholic Record Society 9, 1911, 1-11.

9. DIRECTORIES, MAPS AND DIALECT.

A. Directories

Directories are invaluable sources for locating people in the nineteenth and early twentieth centuries; they are the equivalent of the modern phone book. For brief discussion of Essex directories, see: MATTHEWS, RICHARD. 'Directories of historic Essex', *E.J.* **25**(3), 1990, 64-6 & 74. MATTHEWS, RICHARD M.S. 'Directories of historic Essex', *Romford record* **20**, 1988, 8-11.

Many directories for Essex were published. The following list is selective, based on what I have actually seen; further works may be identified (with locations) by consulting the works listed in Stuart Raymond's *English genealogy: a bibliography*. It may be noted that many London directories covered suburban parishes in Essex. The following citations are arranged chronologically and by place (although place may conceal coverage of a much wider area than is apparent from directory titles).

Pigot and Co.'s London & provincial new commercial directory for 1828-9 ... in addition to which is compiled, with greatest care, a directory of the County of Middlesex, with every town and village within twelve miles of the metropolis, and in the counties of Essex, Herfordshire, Kent, Surrey and Sussex ... 3rd ed. J. Pigot & Son, 1828.

Pigot and Co.'s Royal National and Commercial directory and topography of the counties of Bedford, Cambridge, Essex, Herts., Middlesex, Norfolk, Suffolk, Surrey and Sussex comprising classified lists of all persons in trade, and clergy. J. Pigot & Co., 1839. Partially reprinted in facsimile, Kings Lynn: Michael Winton, 1992. Also available on fiche, published by E.S.F.H.

WHITE, WILLIAM. *History, gazetteer and directory of the county of Essex, comprising, under a lucid arrangement of subjects, a general survey of the county, and separate historical, statistical and topographical description of all the hundreds, liberties, unions, boroughs,* *towns, ports, parishes, townships, villages and hamlets* Sheffield: the author, 1848-63, 2 issues. 1848 issue reprinted on 6 fiche as *White's 1848 directory of Essex,* [ ]: E.S.F.H., [199-?]

Post Office directory of Essex, Herts., Middlesex, Kent, Surrey & Sussex. Kelly & Co., 1862-78. 5 issues. Continued by *Kelly's directory of the six home counties.* 2 vols. Kelly & Co., 1882. Continued by: *Kelly's directory of Essex, Hertfordshire and Middlesex.* Kelly & Co., 1887-1933. 15 issues. The Essex portion has also been published with directories for other counties, and separately as: *The Post Office directory of Essex.* Kelly and Co., 1862-78. Continued as *Kelly's directory of Essex.* Kelly & Co., 1882- . Kelly & Co., some issues have been re-published on fiche by E.S.F.H.

Benfleet
Directory of residents and guide to Benfleet, North Benfleet, Canvey Island, Hadleigh, Hockney ... Vange and Wickford. Benfleet: Benfleet, Canvey & District News, 1923. Not seen.

Billericay
The Billericay & Wickford directory and yearbook. Brentwood Gazette & Printing Co., 1923-6. Not seen.

Bocking
See Braintree

Braintree
C. Joscelyne's, Braintree, Bocking & District almanac & directory. Braintree: C. Joscelyne, 1923-6. Not seen.

Brentwood
Brentwood and District directory and year book. Brentwood: Brentwood Gazette Printing Co., 1922-39. Title varies.

Chelmsford
Stevens directory for Chelmsford and neighbourhood. G. Stevens, 1881-94. 2 issues. Not seen.
Chelmsford directory and almanac. Benham & Co., 1910-13. Not seen.
Jewells Chelmsford directory. 1921-2. 2 issues.

Kelly's directory of Chelmsford and neighbourhood. Kelly & Co., 1927-74. Many issues.

Clacton
Line brothers directory for Clacton-on-Sea, Essex. Line Bros., 1888. Not seen.

The Clacton Graphic directory a comprehensive street directory of Clacton-on-Sea and environs Clacton: Clacton Graphic Printing Co., 1902.

The East Essex year book and directories for Clacton and district 4 vols. Clacton: East Essex Printing Works, 1914-17. Continued by: *The Clacton year book and directory.* Clacton: East Essex Printing Works, 1920- .

The Clacton directory & handbook, with directories of Holland-on-Sea, Little Clacton, St. Osyth & Jaywick. Clacton: A. Quick & Co., 1934-47.

Colchester
Benham's almanack and annual advertiser for Colchester and East Essex. Colchester: Benham and Co., 1845-1965. Annual; title varies. Later issues entitled *Benham's Colchester directory.* Earlier issues are less useful, being primarily almanacs rather than directories.

Cullingford's annual, containing complete street, alphabetical and military directories of Colchester. Colchester: R.W. Cullingford, 1887-1915. Annual, title varies.

Colchester almanac for 19--: directory of the town with much local and general information. Colchester: Essex County Telegraph, 1912-40. Many issues; title varies.

The county telegraph almanac, handbook and directory for Colchester and district for 1938. Colchester: County Telegraph, 1938.

Dunmow
Robus Bros. almanack for 1923 with Dunmow directory, notes on the Dunmow charters and gazetteer of the district. Dunmow: Robus Bros., 1923.

Epping
Davis' Epping, Loughton and Ongar almanack 1903, with directories of Epping, Theydon Bois, High Beach, Loughton and Ongar. Epping: Alfred B. Davis, 1903. 40th year of publication, but no others seen.

Grays
Wilson & Whitworth's Grays almanac and yearbook of information, local advertiser, and calender. [ ]: Wilson & Whitworth, 1885-1932. Continued by:

Directory of Grays, Tilbury, Chadwell St. Mary, Little Thurrock, West Thurrock, Purfleet, Stifford, Aveley, Orsett and Stanford le Hope. Wilson & Whitford, 1993-6. Not seen.

Harwich
The Harwich and Dovercourt business and family almanac diary and directory. Harwich: G.L Jackson, 1885.

Ilford
Kellys Ilford, Manor Park, Little Ilford and East Ham directory (buff book) Kelly's Directories 1899-1907. Annual; continued by:

Kellys Ilford, inclusive of Seven Kings and Goodmayes directory (buff book) Kellys Directories, 1909-39. Many issues.

Leytonstone
Kellys Leytonstone, Wanstead and Snaresbrook directory (buff book) Kellys Directories, 1909-39. Many issues; title varies.

Romford
EVANS, BRIAN. 'Late 18th century directories of Romford, 1784 & 1798', *Romford record* 8, 1976, 22-7. Extracts from the *British directory* for 1784 only.

'Trades & professions of Romford 1863: (extracts from White's directory of Essex)', *Romford record* 12, 1980, 40-46.

Wilson & Whitworths Romford almanack, directory, year book of information, local advertiser & calendar. Romford: Wilson & Whitworth, 1902-6. Two issues only seen, 1902 issues states 41st year of publication.

Romford official guide and directory. Gloucester: British Publishing Co., 1924.

Romford intelligence and guide (Borough of Romford official year and record book). Romford: Fletchers, [1938?] Includes street directories.

Saffron Walden
The Saffron Walden and district year book, almanack and directory. Saffron Walden, 1933-9.

Southend
Kellys directory of Southend-on-Sea, Leigh-on-Sea, Westcliff and neighbourhood.
Kellys directories, 1899-1973. 53 issues.
Title varies.

Stratford
Kellys Stratford, West Ham, Leyton, Leytonstone, Forest Gate, Walthamstow & Plaistow directory. Kelly & Co., 1887-1905.
Annual. Title varies.

Walthamstow
Kellys Walthamstow, Leyton & Leytonstone directory (buff book). Kellys Directories, 1886-1908. 22 issues.

West Essex
West Essex Gazette Epping and Loughton directory 1920-1921. Epping: West Essex Gazette, 1920.

Wickford
See Billericay

Woodford
Directory of Woodford, Wanstead, Buckhurst Hill, Chigwell, Loughton and Chingford containing the private and commercial residents. Woodford: James Jones & Sons, 1883-7. 2 issues. Title varies.
Kellys Woodford and Wanstead and Snaresbrook directory (buff book) Kellys Directories 1909-39. Title varies.

B. *Maps and Place-Names*
Many obscure place-names occur in genealogical sources. One way to identify them is to consult a place-name directory.
See:
REANEY, P.H. *The place-names of Essex.*
English Place-Name Society **12.**
Cambridge: C.U.P., 1935.
See also:
O'LEARY. JOHN G. *Dagenham place names.*
Dagenham: Borough of Dagenham, 1958.
A good map is also useful. For a detailed listing of county maps, see:
EMMISON, F.G. *County maps of Essex, 1576-1852: a handlist.* E.R.O. publication **25.** 1955.
TOOLEY, RONALD V. 'Large scale English county maps and plans of cities not printed in atlases part 11: Essex', *Map collector* **36** 1986, 36-8. Catalogue.

Numerous maps are held by Essex Record Office. These are listed in:
EMMISON, F.G. ed. *Catalogue of maps in the Essex Record Office 1566-1855.* E.R.O. publication **3.** 1947. Supplemented by:
EMMISON, F.G., ed. *Catalogue of maps in the Essex Record Office: first supplement.* E.R.O. publication **16.** 1952.
See also:
BRYANT, MARGARET E. *Exhibition of Essex estate, county and official maps held at the South-West Essex Technical College, Walthamstow, March 6-19 1948.* [ ]: Essex Education Committee, 1948.
STEER, FRANCIS W. & HULL, FELIX. *Illustrated handbook to exhibition of Essex estate, county and official maps.* [ ]: Essex Education Committee, 1947.
Reference should also be made to Mason's *Essex on the map;* see above, section 5, 'land surveyors'.
The most useful maps are probably the 1st editions of the Ordnance Survey's one-inch series. This has been reprinted in book format:
The old series Ordnance Survey maps of England and Wales volume 1: Kent, Essex, E. Sussex and S. Suffolk. Lympne Castle: Harry Margary, 1975. Reprinted sheet maps from the original 1″ survey are also available from the publishers David & Charles.
You may need to know the boundaries of registration districts.
See:
MURRELLS, DONOVAN, J. *Registration districts of Essex 1836, with maps and list of parishes.* D.J. Murrells, 1994.
You may also need to know which parishes are next to each other. For a list of contiguous parishes, see:
Essex contiguous parishes. CART Publications, 1997.

C. *Dialect*
If obscure dialect words found in genealogical sources give you problems, you may need to consult a dialect dictionary.
A number are available:
CHARNOCK, RICHARD STEPHEN. *A glossary of the Essex dialect.* Trübner & Co., 1880.

FISHER, JOHN L. *A medieval farming glossary of Latin and English words, taken mainly from Essex records.* National Council of Social Service for the Standing Conference for Local History, 1968.

FORBY, ROBERT. *The vocabulary of East Anglia.* 2 vols. Newton Abbot: David & Charles, 1970. Originally published J.B. Nichols & Son, 1830.

GEPP, EDWARD. *An Essex dialect dictionary.* East Ardsley: S.R. Publishers, 1969. Originally published London: George Routledge & Sons, 1923.

RYE, WALTER. *Glossary of words used in East Anglia, founded on that of Forby.* English Dialect Society, 1895.

A glossary of provincial words used in the county of Essex. London: John Gray Bell, 1851.

10. OFFICIAL LISTS OF NAMES

Governments are keen on listing their subjects, a trait for which genealogists have cause to be thankful, since the lists which result enable us to locate our ancestors in time and place. Domesday book is the earliest general listing of manorial lords, and has recently been re-published in a convenient format:

RUMBLE, A. ed. *Domesday book, 32: Essex.* Chichester: Phillimore, 1983.

A. Tax Lists

Only two county-wide tax lists for Essex the 1327 lay subsidy and the 1662 hearth tax have been published, apart from a very brief list of the payers of the 'Ninth' in 1340/41. There are also a few listings for particular places. Many Essex returns to the subsidy, the land tax, and a variety of other impositions, still await their editors. The lists which are available include:

WARD, JENNIFER C., ed. *The medieval Essex community: the lay subsidy of 1327.* E.R.O. publications **88.** Essex historical documents **1.** 1983.

AUSTEN, F.W. 'The hundred rolls and inquisitions of the nones', *E.Rev.* **53,** 1944, 53-6. Lists payers of the 'ninth', 1340-41.

Essex hearth tax assessments 1662 (with index). 11 fiche. Society of Genealogists, 1990.

Ashdon

COLLINS, TOM. 'An historical peep into Ashdon, part 1: Domesday and the lay subsidy of 1327', *Saffron Walden history* 5(34), 1988, 35-43. Includes names of subsidy payers.

Colchester

RICKWORD, GEORGE. 'Taxation of Colchester A.D. 1296 and 1301', *T.E.A.S.* N.S., **9,** 1906, 126-55. Includes lists of subsidy payers.

Felsted

FRENCH, JOHN. 'Collecting the poll tax at Felstead in 1381', *T.E.A.S.* N.S., **14,** 1918, 209-17. Discussion giving some names.

Hatfield Peverel
CORNWALL, JULIAN. 'The letter of the law: Hatfield Peverel in the lay subsidy of 1524-5', in NEALE, KENNETH, ed. *An Essex tribute: essays presented to Frederick G. Emmison as a tribute to his life and work for Essex history and archives.* Leopards Head Press, 1987, 143-52. Includes a list of taxpayers.

Hinckford Hundred
OMAN, CHARLES. *The great revolt of 1381.* New ed. with introduction by E.B. Fryde, Oxford: Clarendon Press, 1969. Includes poll tax return for Hinckford Hundred, 1381.

Stock
AUSTEN, F.W. 'Hair powder', *E.Rev.* **61**, 1952, 159-60. Return for the hair powder tax, 1797 at Stock, Ramsden Bellhouse and Ramsden Heath.

B. *Loyalty Oaths*
From time to time, governments demand oaths of loyalty from their demand oaths of loyalty from their subjects. The so-called 'protestation' oath was ordered by Parliament in 1641/2, at the outbread of the Civil War; all adult males were required to sign the oath, and many returns are still preserved in the House of Lords Records Office. Only a few returns survive for Essex; there are also a small number of returns for the related 'solemn League and Covenent'. Those which have been published include:

Barnston
CLARK, ANDREW. 'Barnston notes 1641-1649', *E.Rev.* **25**, 1916, 55-69. Discussion of the protestation return 1641/2 and the Covenant of 1643, with transcripts of both, *etc.*
'Protestation roll of Barnston, Essex July 11, 1641', *Manchester genealogist* **5**(3), 1969, 18.
Mc.LACHLAN, M. 'The Solemn Vow and Covenant of Barnston' Essex, July 13, 1643', *Manchester genealogist* **5**(4), 1969, 12. Lists signatories.

Boreham
McLACHLAN, M. Protestation roll of, Boreham, Essex (August 1, 1641)', *Manchester Genealogist* **6**(3), 1970, 11-12. See also above, p27.

Childerditch
'Protestation roll of Childerditch, Essex, Jan 23, 1641', *Manchester genealogist* **5**(4) 1969, 13.

Dengie
[Dengie protestation] *E.Rev.* **32**, 1923, 34-5. Not seen.

Wanstead
'The Wanstead protestation, 1641', *E.A.M.* 1922, 81. Not seen.

C. *The Census*
By far the most useful lists of names are those deriving from the official censuses. However, a few census type listings are available for earlier dates than the official census. Some of them are transcribed in:
Parish census listings 1797-1831. Essex family history series **2**. 3 fiche in wallet. E.R.O. / E.S.F.H., 1996.
For Ardleigh, see also:
ERITH, F.H. *Ardleigh in 1796: its farms, families and local government.* East Berholt: Hugh Tempest Radford, 1978. Transcript of a private census, with many annotations.

1851
A number of indexes to the 1851 census are available, those published by the Essex Society for Family History cover registration districts rather than parishes.
EAST OF LONDON FAMILY HISTORY SOCIETY. *1851 census index series volume 1: Essex.* 4 pts. The Society, 1982-4. Pt. 1. Rainham, Wennington, Hornchurch, Upminster, Cranham, Great Warley. Pt. 2. Havering, Romford, Pt. 3. Dagenham, Great Ilford. Pt. 4. Barking.

Billericay
1851 census index for Essex: Billericay (HO 107/1774). 1 fiche. Brentwood: E.S.F.H., [199-?]

Braintree
1851 census index of Essex: Braintree. HO 107/1785. 2 fiche in folder. Ingatestone: E.S.F.H., [199-].

Chelmsford
1851 census index of Essex: Chelmsford HO107/1775. 1 fiche in folder. Ingatestone: E.S.F.H., [199-].

Colchester
*1851 census index for Essex: Colchester (HO
107/1781).* 2 fiche. Brentwood: E.S.F.H.,
[199-?]

Epping
*1851 census of index of Essex: Epping. HO
107/1770.* 1 fiche. Ingatestone: E.S.F.H.,
[199-?]

Great Baddow
See Writtle

Great Waltham
See Writtle

Harwich
*1851 census index for Essex: Harwich (HO
107/1780).* 1 fiche. E.S.F.H., [199-?].

Lexden
*1851 census index for Essex: Lexden (HO
107/1782).* 2 fiche. Brentwood: E.S.F.H.,
[199-?]

Leyton
*1851 census index of Essex: Leyton &
Walthamstow. HO 107/1769.* 1 fiche in
folder [ ]: E.S.F.H. [199-?]

Maldon
*1851 census index of Essex: Maldon.
HO 107/178.* 2 fiche in folder. Ingatestone:
E.S.F.H., [199-.]

Ongar
*Ongar census index for Essex: Ongar (HO
107/1771).* 1 fiche. Brentwood: E.S.F.H.,
[199-?]

Orsett
*1851 census index for Essex: Orsett (HO
107/1773).* 1 fiche. Brentwood: E.S.F.H.
[199-?]

Rochford
*1851 census index for Essex: Rochford (HO
107/1777).* 1 fiche. Brentwood: E.S.F.H.,
[199-?]

Saffron Walden
*1851 census index of Essex: Saffron Walden.
HO 107/1786.* 2 fiche. In folder.
Ingatestone: E.S.F.H., [199-?]

Tendring
*1851 census index for Essex: Tendring (HO
107/1779).* 1 fiche. Brentwood: E.S.F.H.,
[199-].

Walthamstow
See Leyton

Wanstead
EAST OF LONDON FAMILY HISTORY SOCIETY.
1851 census index series volume 8:
Wanstead and Woodford. 1 fiche. Woodford
Green: East of London F.H.S., 1994.

Witham
*1851 census index of Essex: Witham.
HO 107 / 1783.* 1 fiche in folder.
Ingatestone: E.S.F.H., [199-.]

Woodford
See Wanstead

Writtle
*1851 census index for Essex: Writtle, Great
Waltham and Great Baddow (H.O. 107 /
1776).* Brentwood: E.S.F.H., [199-?]

1881
1881 census surname index: Essex. 104 fiche
Church of Jesus Christ of Latter Day
Saints, 1992. Important.

Newham
BROOKER, JANICE. '1881 census: Newham
(East & West Ham) R.G. 11 1703', *Kent
Family History Society journal*, **5**(8), 1988,
297-9

D. *Landowners Census*
A different type of census was taken in 1873.
Everyone who owned more than one acre
was listed, and the return for Essex was
published as:
'Essex, in *Return of owners of land, 1873*
House of Commons Parliamentary pages
LXXII, 1874, 389-437. Reprinted as:
*Returns of owners of land in Essex 1873:
new domesday book.* 1 fiche in wallet.
Essex family history series 1. E.R.O. /
E.S.F.H., 1996.

11. RECORDS OF NATIONAL AND COUNTY ADMINSTRATION

The archives of national and county government are essential sources for the genealogist, and many are referred to in other sections of this bibliography see, for example, the previous section. Here are listed works which study or abstract miscellaneous documents which have emanated from government administration, together with various lists of office-holders.

A. *National*
A variety of works deal with local aspects of events or institutions at the national level. These include:

MCINTOSH, MARJORIE K. 'Immediate royal justice: the Marshalsea court in Havering 1358', **54**, *Speculum* 1979, 727-33. The court theoretically heard cases involving members of the royal household, but in practice many local cases were heard whilst it sat at Havering.

BULLEN, R. FREEMAN. 'Essex notes from the Calendar of French rolls, reign of Henry VI', *East Anglian* N.S. **13**, 1909-10, 184-7 & 216-20. Giving names of many granted protection, licences, etc.

BANNARD, HENRY E. 'Essex committees in the Civil War', *E.Rev.* **45**, 1936, 101-7. Lists Parliamentary committeemen.

SMITH, HAROLD. 'Some Essex parliamentarians', *E.Rev.* **33**, 1924, 149-55. Names of members of the county committee.

BROWNE, A.L. 'King James II's proposed repeal of the penal laws and Test Act in 1688: his questions to the magistrates of Essex, with their answers thereto', *T.E.A.S.* N.S., **23**, 1945-7, 125-32. Includes names of J.P.s; also of those considered fit to be J.P.s or deputy lieutenants.

HOLDSWORTH, J.J. 'Essex in the '15', *E.Rev.* **29**, 1920, 102-8. List of suspected Jacobites, 1715.

B. *Members of Parliament*
A variety of works provide lists or biographical information relating to Members of Parliament, at both national and local levels. For works relating to the whole country, see Raymond's *English genealogy: a bibliography*. Local works include:

'Essex elections', *E.Rev.* **2**, 183, 224-30. List of M.P.s for Essex, Colchester, Maldon and Harwich from 1660.

'Essex elections', *E.Rev.* **3**, 1894, 86. List of M.P.s for all post-1832 constituencies.

Colchester
RICKWORD, GEORGE. 'Members of Parliament for Colchester 1547-[1830]', *E.Rev.* **4**, 1895, 110-22 & 235-45; **5**, 1896, 193-213; **6**, 1897, 171-87; **8**, 1899, 226-41.

Romford
HOPKINS, SUSAN. 'Alphabetical list of local members of Parliament since 1832 and candidates', *Romford record* **10**, 1978, 51-7.

Woodford
'The Parliamentary representation of Woodford', *Woodford and District Historical Society proceedings and transactions* **9**, 1947, 3-6. List of M.P.s, 1832-1945.

C. *Lords Lieutenants*
COLVIN, RICHARD B., SIR. *The lieutenants and keepers of the rolls of the County of Essex*. Whitehead Morris, 1934. Detailed biographies.

FITCH, EDWARD A. 'The Lord-Lieutenants of Essex', *E.Rev.* **7**, 1898, 235-51. List, 16-19th c.

QUINTRELL, B.W., ed. *The Maynard Lieutenancy book*. Historical documents **3**. Chelmsford: Essex Record Office, 1993. Many names.

CLARK, ANDREW. 'A Lieutenancy book for Essex, 1608 to 1631 and 1637 to 1639; *E.Rev.* **17**, 1908, 157-69. General description of a potentially useful source.

D. *Sherriffs*
'High sherriffs of Essex (1760-1893)', *E.Rev.* **2**, 1893, 248-50. List, 1761-1893.

E. *Justices of the Peace*
'Justices of the Peace', *East Anglian* N.S. **3**, 1889-90, 313-6. List for Essex, 1585, with brief biographical notes.

F. Assizes

EMMISON, F.G. 'Calendars of Essex Assize files 1559-1714 and Kings Bench indictments (ancient) 1538-1675', *E.J.* 1, 1966, 126-30. General discussion, also printed in: *Thurrock Historical Society journal* 10, 1966, 15-18.

COCKBURN, J.S., *Calendar of assize records: Essex indictments, Elizabeth I.* H.M.S.O., 1978.

COCKBURN, J.S., *Calendar of assize records: Essex indictments, James I.* H.M.S.O., 1982.

EMMISON, F.G. 'The Elizabeth assize files with particular reference to County of Essex', *Society of Local Archivists bulletin* 13 1954, 2-12.

EMMISON, F.G., & NEWTON, K.C. 'Colchester gaol delivery, 1392 & 1457', *T.E.A.S.* 3rd series 2(3), 1970, 280-88.

G. Quarter Sessions

A full description of the extensive archive of Essex Quarter Sessions is provided in Emmison's guide to the Essex Record Office, listed above, section 3. This supersedes:

EMMISON, F.G. *Guide to the Essex quarter sessions and other official records preserved in the Essex Record Office, Chelmsford.* Occasional publications 2. Colchester: Essex Archaeological Society, 1946.

Other listings include:

JEAFFRESON, JOHN CORDY. 'The manuscripts of the County of Essex', in HISTORICAL MANUSCRIPTS COMMISSION. *The manuscripts of the Earl of Westmorland, Captain Stewart, Lord Stafford, Lord Muncaster and others.* 10th report, appendices, part IV. H.M.S.O. 1885, 466-513.

JEAFFRESON, JOHN CORDY. 'The manuscripts of the custos rotulorum and justices of the peace of the county of Essex, at the Shire-Hall, Chelmsford, Co. Essex', in HISTORICAL MANUSCRIPTS COMMISSION. *Tenth report, appendix, part IV.* H.M.S.O., 1885, 466-513.

DICKEN, E.P. 'A note on the county records at Chelmsford', *T.E.A.S.* N.S., 19, 1936, 288-94. Primarily brief extracts from sessions rolls, 16-17th c.

Examples of many relevant records are provided in:

ROWLEY, N. *Law and order in Essex.* 2nd ed. S.E.A.X. series of teaching portfolios 3. E.R.O. publications 54. [197-?]

A number of editions of Quarter Sessions order books and other records are available:

FURBER, ELIZABETH CHAPIN, ed. *Essex justices of the peace, 1351, 1377-1379.* Occasional publications 3. Colchester: Essex Archaeological Society, 1953.

ALLEN, D.H. *Essex Quarter Sessions order book 1652-1661.* Essex edited texts 1. E.R.O. publications 65. Chelmsford: Essex County Council, 1974.

EMMISON, F.G., ed. *Essex freeholders book 1734: a transcript of Essex Record Office Q/RJ1/1.* Chelmsford: Friends of Historic Essex, 1982. Lists men qualified to serve on juries.

See also

CAM, HELEN M. 'Some early inquests before custodes pacis', *English historical review* 40, 1925, 411-9. Transcript of inquests held in Essex 1277 and 1308.

BRIDGE, H.N. 'Glimpses of local history form the Quarter Sessions of the 16th & 17th centuries', *Transactions of the Southend-on-Sea and District Antiquarian and Historical Society* 4(2), 1951, 84-104.

HOLCROFT, WILLIAM. *William Holcroft his booke: local office holding in late Stuart Essex*, ed. J.A. Sharpe. Essex historical documents 2. E.R.O. publication 90. 1986. Record book of a J.P., tax collector, verderer and militia officer; many names.

SPERLING, C.P.D. 'Essex county accounts, 1709', *East Anglian* N.S. 3 1889-90, 249-51, Includes names of chief constables, etc.

HOWARD, ELIOT. 'A minute book of Essex justices 1757 to 1781', *E.Rev.* 28, 1919, 17-22. Discussion of Becontree Hundred manuscript.

H. Poor Law Record

Poor law records are particularly useful to genealogists. For a good introduction, including examples of many relevant records, see:

ROWLEY, N. *Relief of the poor in Essex.* S.E.A.X. series of teaching portfolios 4. E.R.O. publications 58. 1981.

Settlement examinations conducted under the Poor Law provide much information on our ancestors movements. A name index to Essex settlement papers is available on fiche:

Name index to poor law settlement papers. 3 fiche in wallet. Essex family history series 3. E.R.O. / E.S.F.H., 1996.

Many settlement examinations have been transcribed by Jack Baxter:

BAXTER, JACK H. *Settlement examinations 1720-1844: Rawreth & Rayleigh, Essex. (preserved at the Southend-on-Sea branch of Essex Record Office).* Essex settlement series 2. Benfleet: E.S.F.H., 1985.

BAXTER, JACK H. *Settlement examinations 1724-1843 in South-East Essex (S. Benfleet, Canewdon, Hodleigh, Prittlewell, Sutton, Little Wakering) (preserved at the Southend-on-Sea branch of Essex Record Office).* Benfleet: E.S.F.H., 1985.

BAXTER, JACK H. *Settlement examinations 1728-1830, Rockford, Essex. (preserved at the Southend-on-Sea branch of Essex Record Office).* Essex settlement series 1. Benfleet: E.S.F.H., 1985.

For a description of a collection of settlement certificates found in Great Leighs parish chest, see:

CLARK, A. 'Essex labourers certificates 1701-1800', *E.Rev.,* **23**, 1914, 19-27.

Other works on the poor law are listed by place in section 11.

F. *Charity Records*

'Charities and trusts records in Essex Record Office', *Manchester genealogist* **5**(3), 1969, 17. Brief list.

G. *Commissioners of Sewers*

EMMISON, F.G. 'Commissioners of Sewers records', *T.E.A.S.* N.S., **23**, 1945-7, 173-4. Brief discussion of an important but neglected source 1646-1736.

12. RECORDS OF PAROCHIAL AND BOROUGH ADMINISTRATION

The records of parochial and borough government – the accounts of churchwardens and other parish officers, rate lists, poor law records *etc.,* – contain much information of genealogical value. Many works based on them have been published, and are listed here by place.

Aveley
MARTIN, G.T. 'Poor relief at Aveley in the 17th century', *Thurrock Historical Society journal* **2**, 1957, 38-42. Brief discussion.

Barking
COOK, STAN. 'In Barking House of Correction 1820-1823', *C.A.* **53**, 1992, 7-10. Lists inmates.

OXLEY J.E. *Barking vestry minutes and other parish documents.* Colchester: Benham & Co., 1955. Extensive general study.

Benfleet
'Benfleet parish and the poor: the Benfleet & Thundersley Workhouse', *Journal of the Benfleet & District Historical Society* **6**, 1959, 7-13. Includes extracts from accounts, etc., 1799-1820.

Braintree
EMMISON, F.G., ed. *Early Essex town meetings: Braintree 1619-1636; Finchingfield, 1626-1634.* Phillimore, 1970. Transcripts of 'town books'.

CUNNINGTON, HERBERT JOHN. *An account of the charities and charitable benefactions of Braintree.* Elliot Stock, 1904.

Bulphan
LE MAY, DEREK. 'The poor and the sick', *Panorama: the journal of the Thurrock Historical Society* **18**, 1974-5, 7-13. Discussing the operation of the poor law in Bulphan, 18-19th c.

Burnham
'Burnham parish records', *E.Rev.* **29**, 1920, 123-6. Brief extracts from overseers' accounts, 18th c.

DILLIWAY, R. 'Parochial records of Burnham', *E.Rev.* **29**, 1920, 23-6. Brief note on overseers' accounts 1712-60.

Chadwell St.Mary

HAYSTON, J.R. 'The Sleepers Farm papers', *Panorama: the journal of the Thurrock Historic Society* **12**, 1968, 52-67. Notes on Chadwell parish records.

Chelmsford

HUTCHINGS, ANN P. 'The relief of the poor in Chelmsford, 1821-1829', *E. Rev.* **65**, 1956, 42-56. General discussion.

PRESSEY, W.J. 'The churchwardens' book of St. Mary, Chelmsford', *E. Rev.* **48**, 1939, 120-8 & 198-203.

Chingford

'Chingford rate books known to be in existence and their whereabouts', *Chingford notes* **1**(5), 1976, 34.

Colchester

There are a number of reports on the borough's archives:

HARROD, HENRY. *Repertory of the records and evidences of the borough of Colchester.* Colchester: Essex and West Suffolk Gazette, 1865.

HARROD, H. *Report on the records of the borough of Colchester.* Colchester: Essex and West Suffolk Gazzette, 1865.

BENHAM, W. BURNEY. 'The town charters and other borough records of Colchester', *Archaeological journal* **64**, 1907, 203-9.

For court rolls see:

HARROD, HENRY. *Calendar of the court rolls of the Borough of Colchester, with lists of bailiffs and mayors to the present year.* Colchester: Essex and West Suffolk Gazette, 1865.

JEAYES, I.H., ed. *Court rolls of the borough of Colchester.* 4 vols. Colchester Town Council, 1921-41. v.1. 1310-1352. v.2 1353-1367. v.3 1372-1379. v. 4. 1379-83.

Bailiffs and mayors are listed in:

RICKWORD, G. *Bailiffs and mayors of Colchester.* Colchester: Benham and Co., [1903?].

'Complete list of Colchester mayors', *Essex notebook and Suffolk gleaner* **3**, 1884, 25.

For town clerks, see:

ALSFORD, STEPHEN. 'The town clerks of medieval Colchester', *E.A.H.* **24**, 1993, 125-35. General discussion.

Two important medieval documents have been published.

BENHAM, W. GURNEY, ed. *The oath book or red parchment book of Colchester.* Colchester: Essex County Standard office, 1907. Mainly 14-16th c.

BENHAM, W. GURNEY, ed. *The red paper book of Colchester.* Colchester: Essex county Standard Office, 1902. Transcript of a 15th c. council order book.

For the medieval period, see also:

BRITNELL, R.H. 'Bailiffs and burgesses in Colchester, 1400-1525', *E.A.H.* **21**, 1990, 103-9. General discussion.

BRITNELL, R.H. 'Colchester courts and court records, 1310-1525', *E.A.H.* **17**, 1986, 133-40. Municipal politics of nineteenth century Colchester are discussued in:

PHILLIPS, ANDREW. *Ten men and Colchester: public good and private profit in a Victorian town.* E.R.O.publication **89**. 1985.

Colchester Union

HOWLETT, GEOFFREY. 'Workhouse miscellany', *E.A.H.* **47**, 1988, 7; **48**, 1988, 1-19. Includes list of 84 paupers in the Colchester Union workhouses, 1835.

Danbury

HOPKIRK, MARY. 'The administration of poor relief, 1604-1834, illustrated from the parochial records of Danbury', *E.Rev.* **58**, 1949, 113-21.

Dedham

RENDALL, G.H. 'Dedham in the 17th century', *E. Rev.* **39**, 1931, 75-81, 128-32 & 188-90. Includes many extracts from churchwardens' accounts.

Dunmow

MAJENDE, LEWIS A. 'The Dunmow parish accounts', *T.E.A.S.* **2**, 1863, 229-37. Brief extracts, 16th-17th c.

East Ham

DENMAN, HERBERT, ed. *The chronicles of the parish of East Ham, Essex, according to the old minute books, 1735-1867.* Wilson & Whitworth, 1901. Extracts from minute books.

Epping

SWORDER, C.B. 'An Epping charity', *E.Rev.* **14**, 1903, 36-44. Includes extracts from accounts, and will of John Baker of Epping, 1518.

WINSTONE, BENJ. *Extracts from the minutes of the Epping and Ongar Highway Trust from its commencement in 1769 to its termination in 1870.* Harrison and Sons, 1891.

Epping Forest

HUNTER, R. *The Epping Forest Act, 1878, with an introduction, notes, and an index.* Davis and Son, 1878. Includes list of owners and occupiers.

Felsted

GEPP, E. 'Felstead parish book, 1777-1835', *E.Rev.* **29**, 1920, 27-43. General discussion.

Finchingfield

S., C.F. 'Poor relief in Finchingfield 1630', *E.Rev.* **8**, 1899, 128. Minutes of overseers' meeting.
See also Braintree

Great Dunmow

CLARK, ANDREW. 'Church affairs at Great Dunmow', *E.Rev.* **21**, 1912, 73-82. Mainly extracts from churchwardens' accounts.

CLARK, ANDREW. 'Great Dunmow church antiquities 1526-1546', *E.Rev.* **21**, 1912, 141-50. Mainly extracts from churchwardens' accounts.

CLARK, ANDREW. 'Great Dunmow revels, 1526-1543', *E.Rev.* **19**, 1910, 189-98. Includes many extracts from churchwardens' accounts.

Great Hallingbury

WILLIAMS, J.F. 'Great Hallingbury churchwardens' accounts 1526 to 1634', *T.E.A.S.* N.S., **23**, 1945-7, 98-115. General discussion, includes list of churchwardens.

Grays Thurrock

HAYSTON, J.R. 'Grays Thurrock vestry book, 1724-1807', *Panorama: The journal of the Thurrock Historical Society* **14**, 1971, 16-30. General discussion.

HAYSTON, J.R. 'Military service in the French revolutionary wars, with some other incidences of the war in a local parish', *Thurrock Local History Society Journal* **1**, 1956, 12-16. Lists men who paid a guinea to be exempt from service in the militia in Grays and West Thurrock.

Harlow

EDWARDS, F.C. 'Harlow charities', *E.Rev.* **14**, 1905, 169-74.

Harwich

Calendar of muniments in the possession of the Borough of Harwich, with report of the Borough Muniments Committee. Borough of Harwich, 1932.

Heybridge

PRESSEY, W.J. 'The churchwardens' accounts of Heybridge', *T.E.A.S.* N.S., **22**, 1940, 28-36. Brief extracts, 16-17th c.

PRESSEY, W.J., ed. *The first book of churchwardens' accounts of Heybridge, Essex (cir. 1509-1532).* [Heybridge]: [the editor?] [193-?]

PRESSEY, W.J., ed. *The second book of the churchwardens' accounts of Heybridge, Essex.* Ilford: [ ], 1937. Not seen.

High Easter

GEPP, EDWARD. 'High Easter churchwardens' books', 1814-1877', *E.Rev.* **26**, 1917, 101-15. General discussion.

Little Parndon

GLASSCOCK, J.L. 'Gleanings from an Essex parish register', *E.Rev.* **15**, 1906, 25-31. Brief extract from Little Parndon parish register, 17th c., mainly to do with parochial administration rather than vital events.

Maldon

CLARK, ANDREW. 'Maldon civil courts, 1402', *E.Rev.* **16**, 1907, 126-33. General discussion.

Ongar

See Epping

Ramsden Bellhouse

AUSTEN, F.W. 'Churchwardens' disbursements, Ramsden Bellhouse, 1745-1863', *E.Rev.* **55**, 1946, 36-42.

AUSTEN, J.W. 'Overseers' accounts and proceedings in vestry, Ramsden Bellhouse', *E.Rev.* **62**, 1953, 41-6. Brief extracts, 1790-1841.

Rochford Hundred

BAXTER, JACK H. 'Ye have the poor always with you: some observations on the law of settlement in the Rochford Hundred', *E.J.* **23**(2), 1988, 46-7.

CAM, HELEN M. 'Local government in the 13th century, with special reference to Rochford Hundred', *Transactions of the Southend-on-Sea & District Antiquarian & Historical Society* **1**, 1921-2, 65-70. General discussion.

Romford

EVANS, BRIAN. 'The Romford workhouse act 1786 and the thirty directors', *Romford record* **8**, 1976, 14-21. See also 28-9. Includes names of directors of the workhouse.

HOPKINS, SUSAN. 'The Liberty accounts 1835-1843: an introduction', *Romford record* **12**, 1980, 8-14. General discussion.

WHITWOOD, CHARLES J. 'Romford as seen through account and minute books', *Romford record* **2**, 1969, 29-34. Brief extracts from constables' accounts, *etc* ., 19-20th c.

Saffron Walden

HUMPHREYS, DOROTHY. 'Saffron Walden Workhouse: the first thirty years', *Saffron Walden history* **12**, 1977, 94-100. General discussion.

STACEY, H.C. 'Saffron Walden churchwardens accounts', *Saffron Walden history passim* **23**, 1983, 195-8. Brief notes, 17th c.

STACEY, H.C. 'Cataloguing and indexing the corporation archive', *Saffron Walden history* **32**, 1987, 212-7. Of Saffron Walden.

STACEY, H.C. 'Saffron Walden borough cemetery', *Saffron Walden history* **2**(1), 1974 4-15. Administrative history; includes list of board members late 19th c.

STEER, FRANCIS W. 'The statutes of Saffron Walden almshouses', *T.E.A.S.* N.S., **25**(2), 1958 161-221. Includes many names of donors, governors etc., 19th c.

Stanford Rivers

SMITH, HAROLD. 'Stanford Rivers churchwardens' accounts', *E.Rev.* **41**, 1932, 198-9. Brief note, 16-17th c.

Terling

BOUTFLOWER, CHARLES. 'Terling churchwardens' accounts', *E.Rev.* **1**, 1892, 235-9. Brief extracts, 17-18th c.

Theydon Garnon

WALLER, WILLIAM CHAPMAN. 'An old church chest, being notes of the contents of that at Theydon-Garnon, Essex', *T.E.A.S.* N.S., **5**, 1895, 1-32. Includes rental, *temp* Henry VIII, notes on deeds relating to the Garnon or Gernin family, *etc.*

Thundersley

See Benfleet

Walthamstow

BARNS, STEPHEN J. *Walthamstow vestry minutes: churchwardens and overseas accounts 1710-1740.* Official publication, **13**. Walthamstow: Walthamstow Antiquarian Society, 1925. Continued for 1741-1771 in the society's official publication **14**, 1926, and for 1772-1794 in **16**, 1927.

BOSWORTH, GEORGE F. *A history of Walthamstow charities 1487-1920.* Official publication **8**. Walthamstow: Walthamstow Antiquarian Society, 1920.

Wanstead

GRIST, DONALD. *A Victorian charity: the infant orphanage asylum at Wanstead.* R.V. Hatt, 1974. Includes list of children on the establishment, 1832, and many other names.

West Ham

SAINSBURY, FRANK. 'Poor law in West Ham, 1646-1836', *E.J.* **1**, 1966, 163-70. General discussion.

West Thurrock

See Grays Thurrock.

Wivenhoe

BENTON, G. MONTAGU. 'Wivenhoe records', *E.Rev.* **37**, 1928, 156-69. Extracts from churchwardens accounts, 16th c.

R., G. 'Petition of the inhabitants of Wivenhoe', *T.E.A.S.* N.S., **14**, 1918, 186-8. Includes names of 24 petitioners.

Woodford

ERITH, E.J. *Woodford, Essex, 1600-1836: a study of local government in a residential parish.* Woodford and District Historical Society, 1950. Published as the society's *proceedings and transactions* **10**. Includes a list of parish officers, 17-19th c., and of tradesmen 1718-1836.

13. ECCLESIASTICAL RECORDS

A. *Church of England*

The church formerly had a much more important role in society than it has today. The consequence of this fact for the genealogist is that many essential sources – for example, parish registers, probate records, local government records, *etc.* – are to be found in ecclesiastical rather than state archives. Works on ecclesiastical records are listed throughout this bibliography; here, the emphasis is on those topics which are primarily to do with the administration of the church.

For a useful survey of the county's churches (although containing little direct genealogical information), see:

WORLEY, G. *Essex: a directory of the county, mainly ecclesiological.* G.Beth and Sons, 1915.

The records of the two most important archdeaconries are discussed on:

PRESSEY, W.J. 'The records of the Archdeaconries of Essex and Colchester', *T.E.A.S.* N.S., **19**, 1930, 1-21.

Works on church bells and plate provide some information of genealogical value:

BENTON, G. MONTAGUE, GALPIN, F.W., & PRESSEY, W.J. *The church plate of the county of Essex.* Colchester: Benham & Co., 1926.

DEEDES, CECIL, & WALTERS, HENRY BEAUCHAMP. *The church bells of Essex: their founders, inscriptions, traditions and uses.* Aberdeen: the Authors, 1909. Extensive.

DEEDES, CECIL, & WELLS, E.J. 'The church bells of Essex', *E.Rev.* **1**, 1892, 163-7; **2**, 1893, 105-13, 180-5 & 231-7; **3**, 1894, 64-7, 113-8 & 178-9; **4**, 1895, 180-90; **5**, 1896, 102-6; **6**, 1897, 44-8 & 144-8; **7**, 1898, 230-35.

For the medieval period, the bishops' registers provide an important source for diocesan history, and for the genealogist. Three have been edited:

FOWLER, R.C. 'Fulk Basset's register and the Norwich taxation', *T.E.A.S.* N.S. **18**, 1928, 15-26 & 119-34. Transcript of part of a bishop's register, identifiying patrons of livings, mid-13th c.

FOWLER, R.C., ed. *Registrum Radulphi Baldock, Gilberti Segrave, Ricardi Newport, et Stephani Gravesend, episcoporum Londoniensium, A.D. MCCCIV-MCCCXXXVIII.* Canterbury and York Society 7, 1911. Includes extensive register of institutions, 1321-39.

FOWLER, R.C., ed. *Registrum Simonis de Sudburia, Diocesis Londoniensis A.D. 1362-1375.* 2 vols. Canterbury and York Society 34 & 38. 1927-38.

A variety of other works on the church are also available; they are listed here in rough chronological order.

HALE, W.H. *A series of precedents and proceedings in ecclesiastical causes, extending from the year 1475 to 1640, extracted from the Act Books of ecclesiastical courts in the Diocese of London.* F.J. Rivington, Reprinted with introduction by R.W. Dunning, Edinburgh: Bratton Publishing, 1973. Indexed (with some abstracts) in

SMITH, HAROLD. 'Hale's *precedents and proceedings',* *T.E.A.S.* N.S., 19, 1920, 305-10.

PRESSEY, W.H.J. 'The Essex churchwarden (as seen in the Archdeaconry records)', *E.Rev.* 51, 1942, 145-51 & 200-4. Many names of churchwardens, 16-17th c.

KING, H.W. 'Inventories of church goods 6th Edw VI'. *T.E.A.S.* 4, 1869, 197-234; 5, 1873, 116-35, 219-42 & 273-80; N.S., 1, 1878, 5-32; 2, 1884, 165-88 & 223.50; 3, 1889, 36-63. Transcripts of the few that survive; they give names of clergy, churchwardens, *etc.*

FOWLER, R.C. 'Church goods of Essex', *T.E.A.S.* N.S., 10, 1909, 228-36. More Edwardian inventories.

WALLER, WILLIAM CHAPMAN. 'Inventories of church goods, 6 Edward VI', *T.E.A.S.* N.S., 11, 1911, 90-97, 202-10 & 310-20.

DICKIN, EDWARD PERCIVAL. 'Embezzled church goods of Essex', *T.E.A.S.* 13, 1915, 157-71. See also 311. Returns of goods sold prior to 1548, with names of churchwardens.

GRIEVE, HILDA E.P. 'The deprived married clergy in Essex', 1553-61', *Transactions of the Royal Historical Society* 4th series 22, 1940, 141-69.

LOADES, D.M. 'The Essex inquisitions of 1556', *Bulletin of the Institute of Historical Research* 35, 1962, 87-97. Return of persons who had fled the threat of Marian persecution for their protestantism.

BROWNE, ROBERT H. 'Essex churches', *E.Rev.* 15, 1906, 40-49. 16-17th c. extracts from act books and visitation records.

USHER, ROLAND G., ed. *The Presbyterian movement in the reign of Queen Elizabeth, as illustrated by the minute book of the Dedham classis, 1582-1589.* Camden 3rd series 8. Royal Historical Society, 1905. Includes 'a list of puritan ministers concerned in the classical movement', which includes many clergy from the Midlands and East Anglia, *etc.*

SMITH, HAROLD. *The ecclesiastical history of Essex under the Long Parliament and Commonwealth.* Colchester: Benham and Company, [190-?]. Extensive; many extracts from original sources.

PRESSEY, W.J. 'Visitations held in the Archdeaconry of Essex in 1683', *T.E.A.S.* N.S., 19, 1930, 260-76; 20, 1933, 216-42; 21, 1937, 100-119 & 306-26; 22, 1940, 113-25 & 316-29; 23, 1945-7, 145-64. Abstracts, giving names of clergy, churchwardens, *etc.*

HEWITT, GORDON. *A history of the diocese of Chelmsford: a history of the first seventy years of the Anglican Diocese of Chelmsford, from 1914-1984, and including an account of earlier Christianity in Essex and East London.* Chelmsford: Chelmsford Diocesan Board of Finance, 1984.

Clergy Lists

There have been two major attempts to list the clergy of Essex. They are:

HENNESSY, GEORGE. *Novum repertorium ecclesiasticum parochiale Londinensis, or, London diocesan clergy succession from the earliest times to the year 1898.* Swan Sorrenchein, 1898.

NEWCOURT, RIC. *Repertorium ecclesiasticum parochiale Londinense: an ecclesiastical parochial history of the Diocese of London.* 2 vols. Chris Bateman, *et al.*, 1708-10. v. 2. Essex. Includes much biographical information.

A number of authors have identified omissions to Newcourt's work:

REANEY, P.H. 'Early Essex clergy', *E.Rev.* 46-55, 1937-46, *passim.* See also 63, 1954, 188; 3rd series 1(4,) 1965, 24952.

SMITH, HAROLD. 'Some omissions in Newcourt's *Repertorium',* *T.E.A.S.,* N.S., 17, 1926, 23-7 & 267. Early 17th c.

SMITH, J.C. CHALLENOR. 'Some additions to Newcourt's *Repertorium,* volume II', *T.E.A.S.* N.S., 6, 1898, 126-45, 228-57 & 298-326; 7, 1900, 40-64, 153-76, 272-84 & 356-68.

A number of other clergy lists, *etc,* are also available:

'Heads of Essex religious houses', *T.E.A.S.* N.S., 11, 1911, 49-52 & 367-8. See also 17, 1926, 47-8. Supplements list in the *Victoria County History* (see section 1 above).

WALCOTT, E.C. 'Monasteries of Essex', *T.E.A.S.* N.S., 1, 1878, 133-41. Extracts from surrenders, *etc.,* of 1534, listing some of the dispossessed monks.

PRESSEY, W.J. 'State of the church in Essex in 1563', *E.Rev.* 46, 1937, 144-57. Includes list of clergy.

NOLAN, M.M. 'Essex incumbents ...', *E.Rec* 15, 1973, 95-9. Lists 99 clergy who were deprived, ejected or resigned in the years following 1559.

SMITH, HAROLD. 'Appointments to Essex benefices by Commissions of the Great Seal, 1649-1654', *T.E.A.S.* N.S., 18, 1928, 1024. List of ecclesiastical appointments.

SMITH, HAROLD. 'Sources for lists of Essex clergy under the Long Parliament and the Commonwealth', *E.Rev.* 30, 1921, 170-77.

SMITH, HAROLD. 'Some Essex royalist clergy-and others', *E.Rev.* 33, 1924, 80-86.

SMITH, HAROLD. 'The Presbyterian organisation of Essex', *E.Rev.* 32, 1923, 173-9. Lists clergy, c.1645.

SMITH, HAROLD. 'The associated ministers of Essex', *E.Rev.* 29, 1920, 127-31. Some names of Essex clergy in mid 1650s.

SMITH, HAROLD F. 'Admission to Essex livings by the *triers',* *T.E.A.S.* N.S., 20, 1933, 199-210. Clergy admissions, 1654-9.

SMITH, HAROLD, & HOPE, T.M. 'Essex clergy in 1661', *T.E.A.S.* N.S., 21, 1937, 73-83. List drawn up immediatley prior to the restoration.

GRIGSON, FRANCIS. 'East Anglian institutions to benefices', *East Anglian* N.S., 1, 1885-6, 71-2, 89-91 & 105-7. For Cambridgeshire, Essex, Norfolk and Suffolk, by the Vicar General or the Archbishop of Canterbury, 1660-1838.

B. Local Church of England Records

Aveley
GOODES, AUBREY. 'Aveley rectors and vicars', *E.Rev.* 29, 1920, 159-63. List, 1311-1907.

Barking Abbey
LOFTUS, ERNEST A., & CHETTLE, HENRY. F. *A history of Barking Abbey.* Wilson and Whitworth, 1954. Includes lists of abbesses and stewards.

Bocking
B., H.D.S. 'The note-books of a curate of Bocking, 1737-1770', *E.Rev.* 64, 1955, 19-23. Discussion of a book detailing fees, Easter offerings, *etc.*

Bocking Deanery
HOFFMAN, ANN. *Bocking Deanery: the story of an Essex peculiar.* Phillimore, 1976.

Braintree
KENWORTHY, J.W. 'St Michael's church, Braintree, Essex', *T.E.A.S.* N.S., 4, 1893, 254-77. Includes list of vicars and patrons.

Chelmsford
PALMER, C.F. 'The friar preachers, or blackfriars, of Chelmsford', *Reliquary* N.S., 3, 1889, 141-4. Includes notes on benefactors.

Chignal Smealey
CHANCELLOR, FRED. 'Essex churches XIII: St Nicholas, Chignal Smealey', *E.Rev.* 4, 1895, 79-91. Includes list of rectors, with brief notes on monumental inscriptions and the parish register.

Colchester
BENHAM, W. GURNEY, SIR. *Historical notes about the churches of All Saints and St. Nicholas cum St Runwald, Colchester.* [ ], 1934. Brief; includes list of rectors, notes on inscriptions, *etc.*

REID, ELEANOR J.B. 'Lollards at Colchester in 1414', *English historical review* **29**, 1914, 101-4. Transcript of an inquisition, with names.

RICKWORD, GEORGE. 'The obits of the abbots of Colchester', *T.E.A.S.* N.S., **16**, 1923, 122-6. Lists abbots.

Colchester Deanery

RICKWORD, GEORGE. 'Visitation of the Rural Deanery of Colchester in 1633', *T.E.A.S.* **11**, 1911, 36-48. Includes names of clergy and churchwardens.

Danbury

CHANCELLOR, FRED. 'Essex churches IV: St John the Baptist's, Danbury', *E.Rev.* **2**, 1893, 17-32. Includes list of rectors, with brief list of monuments.

Dedham

BROOKS, C.ATTFIELD. *The Dedham lectureship established 1577.* Colchester: C.A.Brooks, 1983. Biographical notes on 'lecturers', i.e.clergy holding the lectureship.

Felsted

CRAZE, MICHAEL. 'Five seventeenth-century vicars of Felstead', *E.Rev.* **60**, 1951, 153-60.

Fryerning

'Extracts from minute books of Essex Archdeaconry Court in 16th & 17th century', *Ingatestone and Fryerning Historical and Archaeological Society transactions* **17**, 1979, 14-15. Relating to Fryerning, 1591-1613.

Great Dunmow

CLARK, ANDREW. 'Great Dunmow bells, 1526-1595', *E.Rev.* **23**, 1914, 127-34. Includes extracts from churchwardens' accounts.

Great Leighs

CHANCELLOR, FRED. 'Essex churches VII: St Mary the Virgin, Great Leighs', *E.Rev.* **2**, 1893, 205-23. See also **3**, 1894, 202-3. Includes list of rectors, brief notes on monuments, *etc.*

CLARK, ANDREW. 'Lincoln College incumbents', *E.Rev.* **19**, 1910, 33-42. Of Great Leighs, 18-19th c.

Great Maplestead

SPERLING, C.F.D. 'Vicars of Great Maplestead', *E.Rev.* **22**, 1913, 11-16. 1365-1912.

Great Tey

SPERLING, C.F.D. 'Great Tey churchyard fence', *T.E.A.S.* N.S., **19**, 1930, 123-5. List of those liable to repair the fence in 1668, and early 15th c.

Hatfield Broad Oak

GALPIN, F.W. 'The history of the church of Hatfield Regis or Broad Oak, with some account of the Priory buildings', *T.E.A.S.* N.S., **6**, 1898, 327-45. Includes list of incumbents, 12-19th c., and list of Priory goods sold, mid 16th c (with names of purchasers).

High Easter

CHANCELLOR, FRED. 'Essex churches XII: St Mary the Virgin, High Easter, *E.Rev.* **4**, 1895, 11-25. Includes list of vicars.

Hornchurch Priory

MCINTOSH, MARJORIE K. 'Hornchurch Priory, Essex, 1158/9-1391', *Revue Bénédictine* **95**, 1985, 116-38. General study.

Little Birch

DAVIES, G.M.R., & WEST, A.R. 'The church of St Mary the Virgin, Little Birch', *Colchester Archaeological Group annual bulletin* **25**, 1982, 30-34. Includes list of pre-Restoration rectors.

Little Leighs

CHANCELLOR, FRED. 'Essex churches XIV: St. John the Apostle and Evangelist, Little Leighs', *E.Rev.* **4**, 1895, 146-57. Includes list of rectors, brief notes on inscriptions, and a few extracts from the parish registers.

Little Waltham

SMITH, BRIAN S. 'Little Waltham church goods, c. 1400', *T.E.A.S.* 3rd series 1(2), 1962, 111-13. Inventory of goods, with many names.

Nazeing
WINTERS, WILLIAM. 'Notices of the Pilgrim Fathers: John Elliot and his friends at Nazing', *Transactions of the Royal Historical Society* **10**, 1882, 267-311. Includes list of clergy at Nazeing, 14-19th c.

Pebmarsh
BAYLEY, T.D.S. *Pebmarsh church, Essex*. Oxford University Press, 1946. Includes list of rectors, 13-20th c., notes on charities, wills, *etc.*

Peldon
GOUGH, ANTHONY W. 'The rectors of Peldon', *E.A.H.* **7**, 1975 61-70. Brief biographical notes, 13-20th c.

Purleigh
CHANCELLOR, FRED. 'Essex churches V: All Saints, Purleigh", *E.Rev.* **2**, 1893, 82-96. Includes list of rectors, and notes on monuments, etc.

Ramsden Bellhouse
See Stock

Runwell
CHANCELLOR, FRED. 'Essex churches, XVIII: St Mary the Virgin, Runwell', *E.Rev.* **5**, 1896, 129-42. Includes list of rectors, with a few monumental inscriptions.

Saffron Walden
BENTON, G. MONTAGU. 'The bells and ringing annals of Saffron Walden', *E.Rev.* **30**, 1921, 32-41 & 65-73. Includes extracts from churchwardens accounts, mainly 17-18th c.
'Vicars of Saffron Walden', *T.E.A.S.* N.S., **22**, 1940, 151-4 & 343-5. List, 13-17th c., supplementary to Newcourt's work (see above, p59.).

Salcott
CHANCELLOR, FRED. 'Essex churches X: St Mary, Salcot Wigborough', *E.Rev.* **3**, 1894, 167-78. Includes list of rectors.

South Ockendon
SMITH, HAROLD. 'South Ockendon clergy, 1640-1660', *E.Rev.* **32**, 1923, 8-13.

Stock
AUSTEN, F.W. *Rectors of two Essex parishes and their times (from the 13th century to the 20th century)*. Colchester: Benham & Company, 1943. Stock and Ramsden Bellhouse; extensive.

Thaxted
SYMONDS, G.E. 'Thaxted and it's cutlers' guild', *Reliquary* **5**, 1864-5, 65-72. Includes list of vicars.
SYMONDS, G.E. 'Thaxted church', *T.E.A.S.* N.S., **3**, 1889, 362-6. Includes list of vicars, 14-19th c.

Theydon Garnon
BELL, A.D. 'Some early rectors of All Saints, Theydon Gernon', *E.Rev.* **35**, 1926, 190-203. Medieval-17th c.

Waltham Holy Cross
WINTERS, WILLIAM. 'Notices of the ministers of the church of Waltham Holy Cross', *Transactions of the Royal Historical Society* **8**, 1880, 356-84. Biographical notes, 16- 18th c.

Walthamstow
REANEY, P.H. *The church of St Mary, Walthamstow*, ed. A.D. Law. Monograph (new series) **8**, 1969. Includes list of vicars.

Wendens Ambo
'Wendens Ambo', *E.Rev.* **6**, 1897, 250-51. List of vicars.

Woodford
EMLER, F.G. *A history of the parish church of Woodford in the County of Essex*. Rushden: Stanley Hunt, 1927. Includes notes on clergy, parish clerks, monumental inscriptions, *etc.*

C. *Nonconformity*
For an overview of nonconformist history in Essex, see:
DAVIDS, T.W. *Annals of evangelical nonconformists in Essex, from the time of Wycliffe to the Restoration, with memorials of the Essex ministers who were ejected or silenced in 1600-1662 and brief notices of the Essex churches which originated with their labours.* Jackson, Walford and Hodder, 1863. Extensive; many names.

Much information on Walthamstow nonconformity is contained in:
BATSFORD, M.E. *Non-conformity in Walthamstow.* 2 vols. Monograph (new series) **19 & 22.** Walthamstow Antiquarian Society, 1977-9. Lists each place of worship, giving names of ministers, *etc.*

Baptists
WHITLEY, W.T. *The Baptists of London 1612-1928; their fellowship, their expansion, with notes on their 850 churches.* Kingsgate Press, 1928. Includes brief notes on each church; covers metropolitan Essex.

STACEY, H.C. 'Hill Street Baptist chapel: an account of the trustees for the donation of Robert Cosens, gent, who died 17th December 1728', *Saffron Walden history* **21,** 1982, 145-50. General discussion, with trustees' names.

Congregationalists

Chelmsford
C., H.S. *The old meeting house, Baddowe Lane, Chelmsford.* Chelmsford: J. Dutton, 1927. Brief history of a congregationalist church, which includes a list of burials in the yard.

Coggeshall
DODDS, J.A. 'The story of Congregationalism in Coggeshall', *Transactions of the Congregational History Society* **5,** 191112, 40-51. General study.

Colchester
BLAXILL, E. ALEC. 'The ministers of Lion Walk church, Colchester', *Transactions of the Congregational History Society* **13,** 1937-9. 54-8. Brief biographical notes.
HERRICK, JOSEPH. 'Brief historical sketch of the Church of Christ meeting in Helen's Lane, Colchester', *Transactions of the Congregational History Society* **7,** 1916-18. 254-61. General study.

Epping
WRIGHT, CHARLES. *Nonconformity in Epping: a brief review of three centuries of religious life, and the history of the Congregational Church, 1625-1895.* Harrison and Sons, 1896. Includes a list of burials in the graveyard, 18-19th c.

Upminster
HUTCHINSON, D. *The story of Trinity.* Upminster: Trinity Church, 1991. Brief history of a congregational church; includes list of ministers, 1801-1991.

Huguenots

Thorpe le Soken
WALLER, WILLIAM CHAPMAN. 'The French church of Thorpe le Soken', *Proceedings of the Huguenot Society of London,* **10,** 1912-14, 256-97. See also **11,** 1915-17, 155. Includes list of 'those who shared in the charitable donations, 1699-1763'.

'Huguenots at Thorpe-le-Soken, Essex', *Proceedings of the Huguenot Society of London* **22**(4), 1974, 369-70. Notes on an unpublished genealogical and sociological study.

Latter-Day Saints
PHILLIPS, ANDREW. 'Mormons in Essex 1850-1870', *E.J.* **18**(3), 1983/4, 57-65. Brief general study.

Moravians
BROWN, EDGAR. 'The Moravians in Essex', *E.Rev.* **63,** 1954, 83-6. Brief note.

Quakers

Barking
DAWSON, H.H. *The early records of the monthly meeting of the Society of Friends.* Published as *Barking Historical Society transactions* **1**(1), 1960.

Colchester
FITCH, STANLEY HENRY GLASS. *Colchester Quakers.* Colchester: Stanley G. Johnson, 1962. Includes an alphabetical listing of births, marriages, and deaths of persons connected with Colchester meetings, from various sources.

Roman Catholicism
Roman Catholics in Essex − 'recusants' to the authorities − have been the subject of much research, due largely to the influence of the Essex Recusant Society. Much of this research, which includes many transcripts of original sources, has been published in that society's journal:

Essex Recusant: journal of the Essex Recusant Society. Brentwood: The Society, 1959-85. This is indexed in: 'The cumulative index to 20 years of research', *E.Rec.* **20**, 1978, unpaginated. Many works relevant to Essex Roman Catholics are listed in Raymond's *English genealogy: a bibliography,* section 14J, including, for example, lists of registers, sources of information on recusant rolls, bibliographies, *etc.* These works are, of course, national in scope, and are not further listed here.

General articles specific to Esssex, and of potential genealogical relevance, include (in rough chronological order):

FOLEY, B.C. 'The breaking of the storm', *E. Rec.* 3(1), 1961, 1-21. Brief study of early recusancy.

CLARK, DOROTHY M. 'Recusants out of prison', *E. Rec.* 4(1), 1962, 41-3. Brief list, 16th c.

CAMPBELL, JOSEPH MARY & NICHOLAS, MOTHER. 'P.R.O. E377/57: Essex recusants in an Exchequer document, 1382-1642', *E. Rec.* **1**, 1959, 51-61 & 104-109; 3(1), 1961, 24-30; 3(2), 1961, 80-83; 3(3), 1961, 124-8; 4(1), 1962, 15-24; 4(2), 1962, 71-6; 4(3), 1962, 111-15; 5(1), 1963, 27-9; 6(3), 1964, 905; 7(1), 1965, 36-9.

MARY CATHERINE, SISTER. 'Essex Quarter session rolls 15561650', *E.Rec.* **8**, 1966, 87-94; **9**, 1967, 60-66. Discussion of uses for recusant history, with extracts and lists of names.

CATHERINE, SISTER, & NOLAN, M. 'The history of recusants as illustrated from the Essex Quarter Sessions, 1575-1650', *E.Rec.* **17-25/6**, 1975-83, *passim.*

O'DWYER, MICHAEL. 'Some Essex recusants of the professional classes, 1580-1600', *E.Rec.* **21**, 1979, 22-36. Discussion.

CATHERINE, MARY. 'Essex recusants at Chelmsford Quarter Sessions July 1586', *E. Rec.* **1**, 1959, 75-7 & 87-93. List.

SHANAHAN, D. 'The penal laws and how they worked', *E.Rec.* **14**, 1972, 53-61. Lists Essex names in recusant rolls of 1592-6, with notes on Waylett, Jennings, Barton and Winterfludd.

O'LEARY, JOHN G. 'Records and recusancy in Essex', *E.Rec.* **13**, 1971, 7-16. Discussion of the 1593-4 recusant roll.

O'DWYER, MICHAEL. 'The distribution of Essex recusants throughout the county', *E. Rec.* 5(3), 1963, 77-90. 16th c. study.

O'DWYER, MICHAEL. 'Recusant wives in Essex', *E.Rec.* **9**, 1967, 43-60. Late 16th c.

CAMPBELL, JOSEPH MARY, MOTHER. 'The Bishop of London's list of Essex recusants in 1605', *E. Rec.* 2(3), 1960, 113-27.

ELLIOTT, N.C. 'The Roman Catholic community in Essex, 1625-1701', *E.Rec.* **25/6**, 1983, 1-70; **27**, 1985, 1-72. Includes pedigrees of Appleton, Atslow and Church, Darcy and Savage, Waldegrave, Whitbred and Wiseman; also useful bibliography.

CAMPBELL, JOSEPH MARY. 'Estreats of fines imposed at Chelmsford Quarter Session 1641-1642', *E. Rec.* **1**, 1959, 25-32. Lists those fined.

KNELL, P.R. 'Essex recusants sequestered during the Civil War and Interregnum', *E.Rec.* **9**, 1967, 1-18; **10**, 1968, 21-7 & 111-16; **12**, 1970, 14-22.

FOLEY, B.C. 'A late seventeenth century report on Essex papists', *E. Rec.* **2**, 1960, 11-12. List of Papists in 1680.

WORRALL, E.S. 'Popish recusants presented in the Archdeaconry of Essex, 1681', *E.Rec.* **16**, 1974, 66-8. List.

HUELIN, GORDON. 'Some 18th century Roman Catholic recusants', *Journal of ecclesiastical history* **7**, 1956, 61-8. Discussion of 'certificates as to Papists' for London and Essex, 1706.

COVERDALE, PHILIP. 'The number of Essex Papists in 1706', *E. Rec.* **2**, 1960, 16-29. Notes on Papists by parish.

HARTHARN, M.J. 'Some Essex recusants in the '15', *E.Rec.* **16**, 1974, 21-5. Includes lists.

O'LEARY, J.G. 'Papist estates', *E. Rec.* 6(2), 1964, 49-56. List of estates registered after the 1715 Jacobite rising.

C., J.L. 'Refusal of Roman Catholics to take the oath of allegiance', *East Anglian* N.S., **7**, 1897-8, 285-8. List of those fined in 1745 in Cambridgeshire, Suffolk, Essex and Norfolk.

WORRALL, J.S. 'Just where did they live?' *E.Rec.* Includes lists of papists at Orsett, Stock, Buttsbury, Ramsden Crays, Chelmsford, Margaretting, *etc.* in 1767.

WORRALL, EDW. S. 'The Essex register of oaths subscribed under the Catholic Relief Act 1778', *E. Rec.* **6**(1), 1963, 17-27. Discussion, including some entries.

WORRAL, EDW. W. 'The Essex register of oaths subscribed under the Catholic Relief Act, 1791', *E. Rec.* **6**(2), 1964, 57-65. Discussion with some names.

ANSTRUTHER, GODFREY. 'Deaths in Essex in 19th century', *E.Rec.* **20**, 1978, 68-74. Late 19th c. Catholics.

OWEN, JOHN. 'Growth of the Essex Catholic community, (1850-1950)', *E.Rec.* **22**, 1980, 1-38.

ANSTRUTHER, GODFREY. 'Converts to Rome', *E.Rec.* **21**, 1979, 48-56; **23**, 1981, 81-4. Biographical dictionary.

A number of articles deal with monks and clergy, *etc.*:

HARTHARN, M.J. 'The Benedictines and post-Reformation Essex', *E. Rec.* **2**, 1960, 32-8. Not completed. Includes biographical notes.

'Inconstant hearts: seminary priests in Essex parsonages', *E. Rec.* **3**(2), 1961, 66-71. Names Roman Catholic priests who conformed, 16-17th c.

KNELL, P.R.P. 'Notes on some 17th century priests in Essex', *E.Rec.* **12**, 1970, 100-105. Includes will of James Thoroughgood, of Bulmers, 1671.

WORRALL, EDW. S. 'Essex families and the Canonesses Regular of the Holy Sepulchre of Liege and New Hall, Boreham', *E. Rec.* **4**(2), 1962, 77-81. Discussion of nuns' family origins, 17-18th c.

WORRALL, EDW. S. 'Eighteenth century Jesuit priests in Essex', *E. Rec.* **4**, 1962, 116-20; **5**, 1963, 34-7, 69-75 & 93-8.

WORRALL, E.S. 'Essex names in the Hammersmith Convent Register', *E.Rec.* **12**, 1970, 62-7. Identifies Essex nuns.

ASHTON, RICHARD. 'Four centuries of the Venerable English College', *E.Rec.* **20**, 1978, 57-61. At Rome. Lists Essex alumni.

Becontree Hundred

WORRAL, EDW. S. 'Catholics in the Becontree Hundred in the eighteenth century', *E. Rec.* **3**(1), 1961, 93-100. Includes various lists of names.

Colchester

WORRALL, EDW. S. 'Colchester papists in the eighteenth century', *E.Rec.* **10**, 1968, 37-41.

Ingatestone

CLUTTON, GEORGE, SIR. 'The chaplains at Ingatestone and Thorndon, 1707-1742', *E.Rec.* **12**, 1970, 106-16. Includes list.

Witham Place

WORRAL, EDW. S. 'The congregation of the Witham Place chapel, 1766-1800', *E.Rec.* **4**(1), 1962, 5-12. Includes lists of 1767 and 1780.

14. ESTATE RECORDS.

A. General

The records of estate administration constitute a mine of information for the genealogist. Much is in print, although much more lies untouched in the archives. The major general work on Essex estate papers is the edition of the feet of fines by R.E.G. Kirk, *et al.* 'Feet of fines' is the curious name for deeds which were entered in the rolls of the Court of Common Pleas. Kirk's edition makes it much easier to trace medieval descents down to 1603.

KIRK, R.E.G., et al, eds. *Feet of fines for Essex.* 6 vols. Colchester: Essex Archaeological Society, 1899-1993. Contents:
v 1. 1182-1272, ed. R.E.G. Kirk.
v 2. 1272-1326, ed. P.H. Reaney & Marc Fitch.
v.3. 1327-1422.
v.4. 1423-1547, ed. P.H. Reaney & Marc Fitch.
v 5. 1547-1580, ed. Marc Fitch & Frederick Emmison. (published Oxford: Leopards Head Press, 1991.)
v.6. 1581-1603, ed. F.G. Emmison. (published Oxford: Leopards Head Press, 1993.)

Later feet of fines are calendered in:
'A calender of the feet of fines for Essex', *East Anglian* N.S., **5-11**, 1893-1906, *passim.* For 1600-1611.

For discussion of the feet of fines, see:
BULLOCK, LL.C. WATSON. 'Comments on the feet of fines for Essex', *E.Rev.* **43**, 1934, 133-6. See also **45**, 1936, 26-30.
JONES, IAN K. 'Essex feet of fines', *The North Middlesex: Journal of the North Middlesex F.H.S.* **4**(1), 1981, 81-2. Originally published in: *Bulletin of the Enfield Archaeological Society* 1981.

The British Library (formerly the British Museum) has extensive collections of estate archives. Manorial court rolls in this collection for Essex, Norfolk and Suffolk are listed in:

STEDMAN, ARTHUR E. 'East Anglian manor court rolls: Mss. Department of the British Museum', *East Anglian* N.S. **13**, 1909-10, 22-4.

Two articles provide abstracts of deeds in a bookseller's collection:
'Paleography, genealogy and topography, *Topographical quarterly* **5**(4), 1937, 221-91.
'The value of old parchment deeds in genealogical and topographical research', *Topographical quarterly* **3**(3), 1935, 173-201.

Other general works include:
'Essex marriage settlements', *E.A.M.,* 1931, 12, 13, 15, 23 & 28-30. Abstracts of ten deeds.
HART, CYRIL. *The early charters of Essex: the Norman period.* Dept. of English Local History occasional papers **11**. Leicester: University Press, 1957. Calendars all surviving Essex deeds, 1066-99.

B. Private Estates

The larger proprietors of Essex had lands in various parts of the county, and sometimes in other counties as well. The estate papers of a number of families have been calendared and published; these and other works on private estates are entered here.

Barrington

BRIGGS, NANCY. 'The Barrington archives, Essex Record Office', Bulletin of the National Register of Archives **14**, 1967, 19-21. Brief description of estate records, mainly medieval.
BRIGGS, NANCY. 'Additions to the Barrington Archives', *T.E.A.S.* **25**(2), 1958, 268-9. Brief note.
EMMISON, F.G. 'Reconstruction of an estate archive', *Archives* **8**(39), 1968, 130-32. Includes brief listing of Barrington family estate papers relating to Hatfield Broad Oak and Hatfield Priory, *etc.*
HORWOOD, ALFRED J. 'The manuscripts of Geo. Alan Lowndes, esq' of Barrington Hall, Co. Essex', in HISTORICAL MANUSCRIPTS COMMISSION. *Seventh report ... Part 1. Report and appendix. C.2340* H.M.S.O.; 1879, 537-89. Lists estate papers of the Barrington family.

Capell
'The manuscripts of the Earl of Essex preserved at the Cassiobury Park, Watford', in HISTORICAL MANUSCRIPTS COMMISSION. *Report on manuscripts in various collections vol vii.* CD.6722. H.M.S.O., 1914, 297-350. Papers relating to the estates of the Capell family in Hertfordshire, Essex and Norfolk, *etc.*, medieval – 17th c.

Cooper
Genealogical abstracts of some of the documents in the possession of Edward Cooper of Great Oakley, Essex. Frederick Arthur Crisp, 1886. Abstracts court rolls of Great Oakley, Little Oakley, Moze, Skighaw, Weeks, *etc.*

Cornwallis
JEAFFRESON, JOHN CORDY. 'Manuscripts still or recently in the possesion of Lord Braybrooke of Braybrooke, at Audley End, Saffron Walden', in HISTORICAL MANUSCRIPTS COMMISSION. *Eighteenth report ... Appendix, part 1 (section II).* H.M.S.O., 1881, 277-92. Includes listing of estate papers of Cornwallis family.

Fraunceys
See Pyel

Harlakenden
STEINMAN, G. STEINMAN. 'Deeds of the family of Harlakenden', *Topographer and genealogist* **2**, 1853, 215-23. 17th c.

Maxey
N., J.G. 'Indenture relative to the family of Maxey and to various lands in Essex', *Collectanea topographica et genealogica* **2**, 1835, 245-6. 16th c.

Petre
FISHER, J.L. 'The Petre documents', *T.E.A.S.* N.S., **23**, 1945-7, 66-97. Discussion of an important family archive, mainly medieval-16th c.

FOSTER STEWART. 'The Petre family archives', *Catholic archives* **5**, 1985, 39-43. Of Ingatestone Hall. Brief description of estate records.

Pyel
O'CONNOR, S.J., ed. *A calendar of the cartularies of John Pyel and Adam Fraunceys.* Camden 5th series **2**. 1993. 14th c. cartularies relating to lands in Northamptonshire, Essex, London and Middlesex; includes pedigrees.

C.Ecclesiastical Estates, etc.
Ecclesiastical estates were of great importance, especially prior to the Reformation; further, their records had a greater chance of surviving than the records of private families, since they were – and, in some cases, still are – perpetual institutions, for example St. Pauls Cathedral. Incidentally, it is worth noting that much land in Essex was owned by institutions located elsewhere. The deeds of these institutions were frequently collected together into chartularies, some of which have been published. These, together with other ecclesiastical estate records, are listed here.

Barking Abbey
OXLEY, J.E. *The accounts for the destruction of Barking Abbey from 20th June 1542 to 10th June 1543.* Published as *Barking Historical Society Transactions* 1(2), 1961.

OXLEY, J.E. *The account book of the cellaress of Barking Abbey 1535-9.* Published as *Barking Historical Society Transactions* **3**, 1965-8.

Caen Abbey
CHIBNALL, MARJORIE, ed. *Charters and custumals of the Abbey of Holy Trinity, Caen.* Records of social and economic history N.S., **5**. O.U.P. for the British Academy, 1982. Properties included the manor of Felsted in Essex; also other manors in Gloucestershire, Hampshire and Norfolk.

Colchester. Saint Johns Abbey.
FISHER, J.L. 'The leger book of St. Johns Abbey, Colchester', *T.E.A.S.* N.S., **24**, 1951, 77-127. Calendar.

MOORE, STUART A., ed. *Cartularium monasterii S. Johannis Baptiste de Colecestria.* 2 vols. Roxburgh Club **24-5**. 1897.

Clerkenwell. Saint Mary's Nunnery

HASSALL, W.O. 'The Essex properties of the nunnery of St. Mary, Clerkenwell', *T.E.A.S.* N.S., **23**, 1945-7, 18-48. Topographical list of grants *etc.*

Colne Priory

FISHER, JOHN L., ed. *Cartularium Prioratus de Colne.* Occasional Publication **1**. Colchester: Essex Archaeological Society, 1946.

Diocese of London

POOLE, REGINALD LANE. 'The records of the Bishop of London', HISTORICAL MANUSCRIPTS COMMISSION. *Report on manuscripts in various collections.* **7**, Cd.6722. H.M.S.O., 1914, 1-9.

Hornchurch Priory

WESTLAKE, H.F. *Hornchurch Priory: a kalendar of documents in possession of the warden and fellows of New College, Oxford.* Philip Allan, 1923.

Hospitallers

GERVERS, MICHAEL. *The Hospitaller cartulary in the British Library (Cotton ms. Nero E.VI.): a study of the manuscript and its composition, with a critcal edition of two fragments of earlier cartularies for Essex.* Studies and Texts **50**. Toronto: Pontifical Institute of Medieval Studies, 1981. The Hospitallers had extensive lands throughout Essex.

GERVERS, MICHAEL, ed. *The catalogue of the knights of St John of Jerusalem in England: secunda camera: Essex.* Records of social and economic history, N.S. **6**. Oxford University Press for the British Academy, 1982.

Lewes Priory

BUDGEN, W., & SALZMAN, L.F., eds. *The Wiltshire, Devonshire and Dorsetshire portion of the Lewes chartulary, with London and Essex documents from the Surrey portion.* [ ]: Sussex Record Society, 1943.

Oxford. New College

HOBSON, T.F. *A catalogue of manorial documents preserved in the muniment room of New College, Oxford.* Manorial Society Publications **16**. 1929. Abstracts of documents relating to various places throughout England, including Birchanger, Hornchurch, Lindsell, Takeley, Widdington, and Writtle, *etc.*, in Essex.

STEER, FRANCIS W. *The archives of New College, Oxford: a catalogue.* Includes an extensive listing of Essex estate papers, also various other counties.

Ramsey Abbey

BIRCH, W. DE G. 'Historical notes on the manuscripts belonging to Ramsey Abbey', *Journal of the British Archaeological Association* N.S., **5**, 1899, 229-42. Includes list of rolls, deeds *etc.*, for properties in various counties including Essex.

Saint Osyth's Priory

'St. Osyth Priory', *E.Rev.* **30**, 1921, 1-13, 121-7 & 205-21. Ministers' accounts, 1512.

Saint Paul's Cathedral

LYTE, H.C. MAXWELL. 'Report on the manuscripts of the Dean and Chapter of St. Pauls', in HISTORICAL MANUSCRIPTS COMMISSION. *Ninth report ...* C.3773. H.M.S.O., 1883, 1-72. Includes valuable information on Essex estate archives.

GIBBS, MARION, ed. *Early charters of the Cathedral Church of St. Paul, London.* 3rd series **58**. Royal Historical Society, 1939. The cathedral owned much Essex property.

HALE, WILLIAM HALE, ed. *The Domesday of St. Pauls of the year MCCXXII, or, registrum de visitatione maneriorum per Robertum Decanum, and other original documents relating to the manors and churches belonging to the Dean and Chapter of St. Paul's, London, in the twelfth and thirteenth centuries.* Camden Society **69**. 1858. Includes documents relating to Belchamp St. Paul, Wickham St. Paul, Adulvesnasa, Tidwoldington, Tillingham, Barling, Runwell, Norton, Navestock, and Chingford, as well as manors in Hertfordshire, Middlesex and Surrey.

SIMPSON, W. SPARROW, ed. 'Visitations of churches belonging to St. Pauls Cathedral, 1249-1252', in *The Camden Miscellany* **9**. Camden Society N.S., **53**. 1895. Separately paginated. Mainly in Essex and Hertfordshire.

SIMPSON, W. SPARROW, ed. *Visitations of churches belonging to St. Pauls Cathedral in 1297 and in 1458.* Camden Society N.S., **55**. 1895. Mainly in Essex and Hertfordshire.

Stratford Langthorne Abbey

F., K. 'Original documents', *T.E.A.S.* **2**, 1863, 189-94. Brief transcript of the 'Legier' of Stratford Langthorne Abbey, including survey of the manor of Rukholde, mid-16th c.

Takeley Priory

REANEY, PERCY H. 'Takeley Priory records', *T.E.A.S.* N.S., **21**, 1937, 329-30. Brief note on an archive at New College, Oxford.

See also Oxford. New College

Tilty Abbey

WALLER, WILLIAM CHAPMAN. 'Records of Tiltey Abbey: an account of some preserved at Easton Lodge', *T.E.A.S.* N.S., **8**, 1903, 353-62; **9**, 1906, 118-21. Discussion of the abbey's chartulary, *etc.*

Wix Priory

BROOKE, C.N.L. 'Episcopal charters for Wix Priory', in BARNES, PATRICIA M., & SLADE, C.F., etc *A medieval miscellany for Doris May Stenton.* J.W. Ruddock & Sons, 1962, 45-63. 11-12th c.

D. *Local Estate Records*

Many estate papers relating to particular places have been published; these are listed here, together with a few works based on estate records.

Ashen

'Ashen charters', *East Anglian* N.S., **3**, 1889-90, 221-3, 291-4, 305-7, 321-3 & 387-90; **4**, 1891-2, 87-9, 213-5, 290-93 & 330-32; **5**, 1893-4, 11-13, 58-61, 82-4 & 108-11. Medieval.

Barking

OXLEY, J.E. *Barking Abbey rental.* 2 vols. Published as *Barking and District Archaeological Society transactions* 1936-7. Rental of Barking, 1456.

HART, C.J.R. 'Barking town in 1609', *E.Rev.* **59**, 1950, 122-32. Transcript of a manorial survey.

Barringtons Fee

'The manor of Barrington's Fee', *East Anglian* N.S., **5**, 1894, 186-9, 198-200, 232-3 & 261. Latin rental, 1446.

Benfleet

'The manor court', *Journal of the Benfleet and District Historical Society* 1980, 7-9. Brief note on Benfleet manorial records, 15th c.

'Owners and tenants of properties marked on 1840 [tithe] map', *Journal of the Benfleet and District Historical Society* **7**, 1960, 7-13.

Birdbrook

SCHOFIELD, PHILLIPP R. 'The late medieval view of frankpledge and the tithing system: an Essex case study', in RAZI, ZVI, & SMITH, RICHARD, eds. *Medieval society and the manor court.* Oxford: Clarendon Press, 1996, 408-49. Includes 'three frankpledge lists for the manor of Birdbrooke'.

SCHOFIELD, PHILLIPP R. 'Tenurial development and the availability of customary land in a later medieval community', *Economic history review* **49**(2), 1996, 250-67. Birdbrooke; based on manorial court rolls.

Borley

BEAUMONT, G.F. 'The manor of Borley, A.D. 1308', *T.E.A.S.* N.S., **18**, 1928, 254-69. See also **19**, 1930, 60-61. Extent of the manor, naming tenants.

'Extenta manerii de Borle', in CUNNINGHAM, W. *The growth of English industry and commerce during the early and middle ages.* 5th ed. Cambridge: Cambridge University Press, 1915, 576-84. i.e. Borley, 1307-8.

Brightlingsea
DICKIN, E.P. 'Manor court rolls of Brightlingsea, 1640-1659', *E.Rev.* **51**, 1942, 1-8.

Burnham
QUAIFE, JILL. 'Reeve's account of the manor of Burnham, 14-15 Richard II, A.D. 1390-1391', *T.E.A.S.* 3rd series 2(2), 1967, 147-58.

Chatham Hall
CLARK, ANDREW. 'Tithing lists from Essex 1329-1343', *English historical review* **19**, 1904, 715-9. Names from the court rolls of the manor of Chatham Hall, in the parish of Great Waltham.
CLARK, ANDREW. 'Serfdom on an Essex manor, 1308-1378', *English historical review* **20**, 1905, 479-83. Includes discussion of serf marriages on the manor of Chatham Hall, in the parish of Great Waltham.

Chelmsford
EMMISON, F.G. 'A survey of Chelmsford 1591', *T.E.A.S.* N.S., **23**, 1945-7, 133-40. General discussion of a useful source.

Chigwell
WALLER, WILLIAM CHAPMAN. 'Chigwell: a rental and some placenames', *T.E.A.S* N.S., **9**, 1906, 273-9. Early 16th c.

Church Hall
CLARK, ANDREW. 'Church Hall manor, Kelvedon', *E.Rev* **19**, 1910, 139-49. Includes survey, 1293/4.
CLARK, ANDREW. 'Church Hall manor, Kelvedon in 1294', *E.Rev.* **22**, 1913, 139-49. Based on a survey of 1294, naming tenants.

Colchester
B., W.G. 'Notes from Colchester court rolls of 1527-1528', *E.Rev.* **48**, 1938, 91-3.
JEAYES, I.H. 'Court rolls of Colchester', *T.E.A.S.* N.S., **14**, 1918, 81-9. See also **16**, 1923, 144-5. Abstract for 14056.
RICKWORD, GEORGE. 'Essex deeds', *T.E.A.S.* N.S., **13**, 1915, 140-42. Notes on collection of deeds relating to Colchester, 17th c.

Copford Hall
HARRISON, A.D. 'Manor of Copford Hall', *T.E.A.S.* N.S., **22**, 1940, 355-7. Includes extracts from 15-16th c. court rolls.

Earls Colne
FISHER, J.L. 'The Probert documents', *T.E.A.S.* N.S., **23**, 1945-7, 263-72. Discussion of estate papers mainly concerned with Earls Colne.

Earls Fee
NICHOLS, J.F. 'The *compotus* of the manor of Earls Fee, Prittlewell, 1515', *Transactions of Southend on Sea District Antiquarian & Historical Society* 2(1), 1923, 142-5. Names tenants.

East Hall
SIER, L.C. 'Manor of East Hall, East Mersea', *E.Rev.* **54**, 1945, 7-11. Extracts from court rolls, 14-16th c.

Felsted
CLARK, A. 'Copyhold tenure at Felstead, Essex', *English historical review* **27**, 1912, 517-22. Discussion of a 1576 survey.

Fingringhoe
BENHAM, GURNEY, SIR. 'Manorial rolls of Fingringhoe, West Mersea and Pete Hall, 1547 to 1558', *E.Rev.* **50**, 1941, 189-200; **51**, 1942, 32-42 & 88-97.
See also West Mersea

Foulness
'Foulenes Bailiwick: the account of Christopher Davyson ...', *Fragmenta genealogica* **8**, 1902, 1-8. 16th c. accounts of Foulness.

Gaines
N., J.G. 'Particulars of the manor of Gaines in Upminster, Essex, in 1772', *Collectanea topographica et genealogica* **1**, 1874, 331-2.

Gobions
ROE, E.A. 'The manor of Gobions, Romford, Essex, and it's owners', *Genealogists magazine* **6**, 1931-2, 190-3. Descent of manor, 14-20th c.

Great Canfield

ELAND, G., ed. *At the courts of Great Canfield.* Oxford University Press, 1949. Substantial history of the manor, with notes on its records, its lords,its tenants, etc.

Great Dunmow

HULL, FELIX. 'Court rolls of the manor of Great Dunmow, 1382-1507', *E.Rev.* **49**, 1940, 152-7.

Great Henny

'Extracts from the court rolls of the manor of Great Henny, Co. Essex', *Fragmenta genealogica* **8**, 1902, 47. 1682-1801.

Great Tey

ASTLE, THOMAS. 'On the tenures, customs, &c., of his manor of Great Tey', *Archaeologia* **12**, 1796, 24-40. Includes descent of Great Tey and Bacons manors, and of various fiefs within them.

Greenstead

SIER, L.C. 'A rental of Greenstead manor, Colchester', *E.Rev.* **27**, 1918, 140-3 & 174-80. Early 17th c.

Hadleigh Castle

SPARVEL-BAYLY, JOHN A. 'Records relating to Hadleigh Castle', *T.E.A.S.* N.S., **1**, 1878, 86-108. See also 187-91. Includes numerous extracts from 14th c. deeds and accounts.

Harlow

FISHER, J.L. 'The chantry of St. Petronilla at Harlow', *T.E.A.S.* N.S., **23**, 1945-7, 321-30. Includes rental, 1547, and deed abstracts, 1301-67, also list of chaplains.

FISHER, J.L. 'The Harlow cartulary', *T.E.A.S.* N.S., **22**, 1940, 239-71. General discussion with some extracts, includes 'table of holders of virgates and half-virgates', 1287-1431. Harlow was owned by the abbey of Bury St. Edmunds.

Havering

MCINTOSH, MARJORIE. 'The Havering manor court 1350-1600', *Romford record* **11**, 1979, 25-33; **12**, 1980, 30-38. General discussion.

MCINTOSH, MARJORIE KENISTON. 'The privileged villeins of the English ancient demesne', *Viator* **7**, 1976, 295-328. Discussion of villein rights, based on the court rolls of Havering, 13th c.

High Hall

See Walthamstow Toni

Higham Bensted

BOSWORTH, GEORGE F. *The manor of Higham Bensted, Walthamstow.* Official Publication **6**. Walthamstow: Walthamstow Antiquarian Society, 1919. Includes descent and lists of tenants, 1353-4 and 1521-2.

Hutton

SCARGILL-BIRD, S.R., ed. *Custumals of Battle Abbey in the reign of Edward I and Edward II (1283-1312), from mss in the Public Record Office.* Camden Society N.S., **41**. 1887. Includes rental of Hutton, 1283-4.

Lawling

NICHOLS, JOHN F. 'Extent of Lawling A.D. 1310', *T.E.A.S.* N.S., **20**, 1933, 173-98. Lists tenants.

Layer Marney

RICKWORD, GEORGE. 'A rent-roll of Sir Henry Marney of Layer Marney', *T.E.A.S.* **13**, 1915, 92-106. For the manor of Layer Marney, 1499.

Low Hall

BOSWORTH, GEORGE F. *The manors of Low Hall and Salisbury Hall, Walthamstow.* Official publication **7**. Walthamstow: Walthamstow Antiquarian Society, 1920. Includes descent and various lists of tenants.

Lyons Hall

CLARK, ANDREW. 'The manor of Lyons Hall, Great Leighs', *E.Rev.* **12**, 1903, 207-21. Discussion of its records, 17-18th c.

Milton Hall

NICHOLS, J.F. 'Milton Hall: the *compotus* of 1299', *Transactions of Southend-on-Sea District Antiquarian and Historical Society* **2**(2), 1932, 113-67. Includes list of beadles, 1211-1540.

NICHOLS, J.F. 'Milton Hall: the extent of 1309 and an inventory of 1278', *Transactions of Southend-on-Sea & District Antiquarian and Historical Society* 1(2), 1926-8, 70-41. Names tenants.

Nazeing
'Court rolls of Nazing and Waltham Holy Cross', *T.E.A.S.* N.S., **20**, 1933, 297. Brief list of those held in Northampton.

Ongar Hundred
WALLER, WILLIAM CHAPMAN. 'A note on the Hundred of Ongar', *T.E.A.S.* N.S., **9**, 1906, 212-9. Discussion of a 16th c. transcript of court rolls.

Pete Hall
See Fingringhoe

Ramsden Crays
EMMISON, F.G. 'Court rolls of the manor of Ramsden Crays, 1559-1935', *T.E.A.S.* N.S., **22**, 1940, 221-8. General discussion.

Saffron Walden
CROMARTY, DOROTHY. 'Chepyng Walden, 1318-1420: a study from the court rolls', *E.J.* **2**, 1967, 104-13, 122-39 & 181-4. Reprinted in *Saffron Walden history* **3**, 1973, 1973, 10-35.

O'LEARY, J.G. 'Saffron Walden in the year 1605', *Saffron Walden history* **10**, 1976, 58-60. Notes on a survey of 1605 which identifies tenants.

ROWNTREE, C.B. 'House in High Street, next door below the Friends Meeting House', *Saffron Walden history* **5**(37), 1990, 119. Names of owners extracted from deeds, 1731-1883.

STACEY, H.C. 'Title deeds relating to no. 50, High Street, Saffron Walden, purchased by Walter Charles De Barr in 1915', *Saffron Walden history* **5**(34), 1988, 31-34. 20 deeds, 1685-1925.

Salisbury Hall
REANEY, P.H. *The court rolls of Salisbury Hall.* Official publication **36**. Walthamstow Antiquarian Society, 1938. General discussion of 'rolls', 1499-1507, with names of tenants etc.
See also Low Hall

Stambourne
WILLIAMS, J.F. 'A collection of Essex deeds at Queens College, Cambridge', *T.E.A.S.* N.S., **20**, 1933, 78-85. Calendar of 52 deeds, 14-16th c., relating to Stambourne.

Steeple Grange
HOWELL, TED. 'Manor of Steeple Grange, Essex: general court baron and customary court', *E.F.H.* **71**, 1994, 22-4. Extracts from court records, 1788-93.

Takeley
MACAULAY, JANET S.A., & RUSSELL, I.M. 'Colchester Hall (Takeley) charters', *T.E.A.S.* N.S., **22**, 1940, 68-86. Includes calendar of 33 13th c. deeds, *etc.*

Thaxted
NEWTON, K.C. *Thaxted in the fourteenth century: an account of the manor and borough, with translated texts.* E.R.O. publications **33**. 1960. Includes survey, 1393, and several 14th c. accounts.

Theydon Garnon
WALLER, WILLIAM CHAPMAN. 'Some Essex manuscripts, being an account of those belonging to W.S. Chisenhale-Marsh, esq., of Gaynes Park', *T.E.A.S.* N.S., **5**, 1895, 200-225; & **6**, 1898, 101-21. Includes many deed extracts relating to Theydon Garnon.

Thorrington
PARTRIDGE, C. 'A Thorrington rent-roll of 1708 and the Partridge family', *E.Rev.* **23**, 1914, 84-8. Many names of tenants; also notes on Partridge genealogy.

Waltham Holy Cross
WINTERS, WILLIAM. 'Historical notes on some of the ancient manuscripts formerly belonging to the monastic library of Waltham Holy Cross', *Transactions of the Royal Historical Society* **6**, 1877, 203-66. Includes rent roll of Arlesey, Bedfordshire, 1541, notes on Waltham chartularies, list of tenants in Waltham Holy Cross, late 12th c., etc.
See also Nazeing

Walthamstow

BARNS, STEPHEN J. *Calendar of deeds relating to Walthamstow, 1595 to 1890.* Walthamstow Antiquarian Society official publication 11. 1923.

BARNS, STEPHEN J. *Calendar of deeds relating to Walthamstow, 1541 to 1862.* Walthamstow Antiquarian Society official publication 21. 1929.

BARNS, STEPHEN J. *Calendar of deeds relating to Walthamstow 1584 to 1855.* Walthamstow Antiquarian Society, Official publication 33. 1935. Described as 'Third series'. Relatively brief selection of abstracts.

REANEY, P.H. *The court rolls of the Rectory Manor, Walthamstow.* Walthamstow Antiquarian Society, Official Publication 37. 1939. General description, with many extracts.

Walthamstow Toni

BOSWORTH, GEORGE F. *The manor of Walthamstow Toni, or High Hall.* Walthamstow Antiquarian Society, Official publications 1 & 10. 1915-22. Includes list of tenants from an estate map of 1699, with notes on descent of the manor.

West Mersea

BENHAM, W. GURNEY. 'Manorial customs in West Mersea and Fingringhoe', *T.E.A.S.* N.S., **13**, 1915, 78-85. See also 307-9. Includes list of tenants, 1547.
See also Fingringhoe

Wethersfield

WALLER, WILLIAM CHAPMAN. 'The manor of Wethersfield: notes from a court roll, *temp* Richard II', *T.E.A.S.* N.S., **10**, 1909, 246-50.

Wivenhoe

WALLER, WILLIAM CHAPMAN. 'A note on the manor of Wivenhoe', *T.E.A.S.* N.S., **10**, 1909, 320-2. Brief discussion of court roll for 1381.

Woodham Ferrers

EMMISON, F.G. 'Survey of the manor of Woodham Ferrers, 1582', *T.E.A.S.* N.S., **24**, 1951, 6-16. General discussion; no transcript.

Writtle

NEWTON, K.C. *The manor of Writtle: the development of a royal manor in Essex, c.1086-c.1500.* Phillimore, 1970. General study.

NEWTON, K.C. 'A source for medieval population statistics', *Journal of the Society of Archivists* **3**, 1969, 543-6. Discussion based on the Writtle manorial court rolls.

JEAYES, I.H. 'Deeds from a parish chest', *T.E.A.S.* N.S., **19**, 1930, 38-46. Calendar of 33 Writtle deeds, 14-17th c.

JEAYES, I.H. 'The Writtle chantries', *T.E.A.S.* N.S., **14**, 1918 158-65. Surveys, 1548.

Wykes

H., A.J. 'A custumal, A.D. MCCXCVIII, of the manor of Wykes, (in the Hundred of Tendring, Co. Essex), among the muniments of G.A. Lowndes, esq., of Barrington Hall', *T.E.A.S.* N.S., **1**, 1878, 109-15.

E. *Manorial and other Descents*

Many historians have worked out the descents of particular properties. The works listed in section 1 and 2 above include many such descents. See also:

RUSH, JOSEPH ARTHUR. *Seats in Essex, comprising picturesque views of the seats of the noblemen and gentry, with historical and architectural descriptions.* King Sell & Railton, [190-?].

POWELL, W.R. 'The Essex fees of the Honour of Richmond', *T.E.A.S.* 3rd series 1(3), 1964, 179-89. Descent, 11-12th c.

Bacons

See Great Tey

Boreham

P., M. 'New Hall, Boreham', *E. Rev.* **17**, 1908, 57-66 & 121-32. Descent, 1062-1799.

Chingford Hall

BARRY, SEPTIMUS. *Chingford Hall.* Published as *Chingford Historical Society bulletin* **8**. 1973. Descent, 16-20th c.

Colchester Castle

[ROUND, J.H.] *History and antiquities of Colchester Castle.* Colchester: Benham & Co., 1882. Includes descent, 17-19th c.

Colne Engaine
ROUND, J.H. 'The manor of Colne Engaine', *T.E.A.S.* N.S., **8**, 1903, 192-8. Descent, 11-13th c.

Chelmsford. Guy Harlings
CHANCELLOR, FRED. 'Guy Harlings, New Street, Chelmsford', *E.Rev.* **25**, 1916, 151-6. Descent of a house, from title deeds, 15-19th c.

Eastbury
Eastbury Manor House, Barking. Monograph **11**. London Survey Committee, 1917. Includes brief notes on descent.

Epping Place
HOLMES, J.H. 'Epping Place', *T.E.A.S.* N.S., **24**(3), 1960, 329-43. Descent, 16-19th c.

Faulkbourne
ROUND, J.H. 'The descent of Faulkbourne', *T.E.A.S.* N.S., **15**, 1921, 35-59. Medieval-16th c., includes pedigrees of Montgomery, Fortescue, Bourchier, Wiseman, *etc.*

Gerberville
ANDREWS, H.C. 'Gerberville manor, Rainham', *T.E.A.S.* N.S., **21**, 1937, 337-8. Descent, 16-17th c.

Gosfield Hall
BECKETT, J.V. 'Gosfield Hall: a country estate and its owners, 1715-1825', *E.A.H.* **25**, 1994, 185-92. Includes summary pedigree of Nugent and Buckingham.

Great Dunmow
SCOTT, W.T. *Antiquities of an Essex parish, or, pages from the history of Great Dunmow.* H.S.King & Co., 1873. Includes monumental inscriptions, list of clergy, etc.

Great Henny
See Layer de la Haye

Great Maplestead. Dynes Hall
SPERLING, C.F.D. 'Dynes Hall, Great Maplestead', *T.E.A.S.* N.S., **20**, 1933, 1-6. Descent; includes pedigree of Deane, 16-17th c.

Great Myles
CLIFFORD, H. 'The manor of Great Myles's, Kelvedon Hatch', *T.E.A.S.* N.S., **12**, 1913, 109-12. Descent.

Great Tey
ASTLE, THOMAS. 'On the tenures, customs, *etc.,* of his manor of Great Tey', *Archaeologia* **12**, 1796, 24-40. Includes descent of Great Tey and Bacons manors, and of various fiefs within the manor.

Hallingbury
COCKS, HEATHER M.E.M. *The great house of Hallingbury: its place in history.* Great Hallingbury: Great Hallingbury Local History Society, 1988. Includes chapters on the families of Morley, Turnor, and Houblon, with Houblon pedigree.

Hatfield Broad Oak
LOWNDES, G. ALAN. 'The history of Hatfield Broad Oak', *T.E.A.S.* N.S., **1**, 1878, 64-82. Descents of estates.

Horham
KING, H.W. 'The descent of the manor of Horham, and of the family of Cutts', *T.E.A.S.* **4**, 1869, 25-42. Includes folded pedigree of Cutte or Cuttes, 16-17th c.

Ingatestone. Brook Cottage
BARWELL, J. 'Brook Cottage, Green Street', *Ingatestone and Fryerning Historical and Archaeological Society transactions* **14**, 1976, 20-21 & 24. At Ingatestone. Descent.

Jay Wick
WALKER, KENNETH. 'Jay Wick: an ancient Essex farmstead', *E.Rev.* **59**, 1950, 15-24. Descent, medieval - 19th c.

Killegrews
ROUND, J.H. 'Killegrews, alias Shenfields', *T.E.A.S.* N.S., **14**, 1918, 291-7. See also **15**, 1921, 92; **16**, 1923, 95-103. Traces descent, 15-16th c., includes pedigree shewing relationship of Berdefeld, Gedge, and Harris.

Langham. Valley House
SIER, L.C. 'Some owners and occupiers of the Valley House, Langham', *T.E.A.S.* N.S., **10**, 1909, 327-33. Descent, 14-17th c.

Lawford Hall
The Hall of Lawford Hall: records of an Essex house and of its proprietors from the Saxon times to the reign of Henry VIII. Ellis and Elvey, 1891. Extensive descent.

Layer de la Haye
JEFFERS, ROBERT H. 'The manors of Layer de la Haye, Pebmarsh and Great Henny', *E.J.* 4(4), 1969, 178-203. Descent, 16-17th c., especially Tey and Gwynne families.

Leytonstone. Wallwood.
TEMPIE, FREDERICK. 'An account of Wallwood, Leytonstone, from 1200-1960', *T.E.A.S.* 3rd series 1(2), 1962, 114-26. Descent, 15-20th c.

Little Stambridge
KING, H.W. 'Some particulars of the descent of the manor of Little Stambridge, not recorded in Essex history, with an account of the families of Cocke and Bourchier, its former possessors', *T.E.A.S.* N.S., 2, 1884, 190-206. 15-17th c., includes pedigree of Cocke.

Marks
HART, C.J.R. 'The manor of Marks, in Dagenham', *E. Rev.* 58, 1949, 68-81. Descent; includes pedigree of Urswick and Rich, 15-16th c., and detailed list of sources.

Netteswellbury
FISHER, JOHN L. 'The manor of Netteswellbury', *E.Rev.* 36, 1927, 72-8. Descent. Includes pedigree of Martin, 18-19th c.

Ongar Hundred
ROUND, J.H. 'The Honour of Ongar', *T.E.A.S.* N.S., 7, 1900, 14-52. Descent, 11-13th c.

Orsett
COLLINS, E.J.T. *A history of the Orsett estate, 1743-1914.* Thurrock Museums publication 2. Thurrock: Thurrock Borough Council, 1978. Details descent through Baker, Wingfield, and Whitmore, 18-20th c.

Pebmarsh
See Layer de la Haye

Ramsey. Roydon Hall
SIER, L.C. 'The descent of Roydon Hall, Ramsey', *E.Rev.* 50, 1941, 15-18. Medieval - 19th c.

Rayne. Netherhouse
VAUGHAN, ELIZA. 'The title deeds of Netherhouse, or an amicable accommodation', *E. Rev.* 51, 1942, 125-132. Descent of a house at Rayne, 18-19th c.

Rayne. Turners
VAUGHAN, ELIZA. 'The title-deeds of Turners', *E.Rev.* 50, 1941, 79-91. Descent of a house at Rayne.

Romford. Marshalls
DUVALL, J.T. 'Marshalls: the story of a house', *Romford record* 14, 1982, 13-18. Traces descent, 15-20th c.

Saffron Walden. High Street
HEFFER, REUBEN. 'Houses in High Street (formerly Cuckingstool End Street) with their owners' names in 1760, 1823 and 1900', *Saffron Walden history* 5(34), 1988, 44-5.

Shelley
ROUND, J.H. 'The early lords of Shelley', *T.E.A.S.* N.S., 11, 1911, 362-5. Descent, 11-13th c.

Theydon Mount
ROUND, J.H. 'The manor of Theydon Mount', *T.E.A.S.* 12, 1913, 198-202. Descent, 13th c.

Thorrington
ROUND, J.H. 'The descent of Thorrington', *T.E.A.S.* N.S., 8, 1903, 373-4. 12th c.

Waltham Abbey
The history of a Tudor house: an historical, architectural and archaeological study of 41, Sun Street, Waltham Abbey, Essex. Waltham Abbey: Epping Forest District Museumm, 1982. Includes details of owners and tenants.

Walthamstow

BOSWORTH, GEORGE F. *Some Walthamstow houses and their interesting associations.* Walthamstow Antiquarian Society, Official publication 12. 1924. Includes notes on descent.

BOSWORTH, GEORGE F. *More Walthamstow houses and their interesting associations.* Walthamstow Antiquarian Society, Official publication 20. 1928.

BOSWORTH, GEORGE F. *Some more Walthamstow houses and their interesting associations.* Walthamstow Antiquarian Society, Official publication 29. 1933. Includes pedigrees of Barsley, Collard, Forder, Pelly, and Whittingham families, 18-20th c.

West Bergholt. Garlands

MCMASTER, IDA. 'Historical notes on Garlands Farm and Kiln, West Bergholt', *Colchester Archaealogical Group annual bulletin* 21, 1978, 18-23. Includes pedigrees of Bigesby, Nutman and Hurrel, 17-18th c.

West Horndon

ROUND, J.H. 'The descent of West Horndon', *T.E.A.S.* N.S., 12, 1913, 312-4. 14th c.

West Thurrock. Buntings Farm

TURNER, OLIVE. 'A history of Bunting's Farm, West Thurrock, Essex, 1680-1780', *Thurrock Historical Society journal* 5, 1960, 37-46. Descent.

15. EDUCATION

Educational records can be useful in identifying pupils, teachers, governers, benefactors, and others associated with schools. For an overview of Essex education, incorporating many examples of relevant records, see:

ROWLEY, N. *Education in Essex, c. 1710-1910.* SEAX series of teaching portfolios 6. E.R.O. publications 64. 1974.

For a list of schoolmasters licensed between 1787 and 1840, see:

'Licensing of schoolmasters in Essex', *E.F.H.* 68, 1993, 4.

Endowed schools, with the names of benefactors, are listed in:

'Endowed schools of Essex', *E.Rev.* 6, 1897, 105-14. See also 188.

For Essex students at Oxford and Cambridge, reference should be made to the works listed in Raymond's *English genealogy: a bibliography.* See also:

CLARK, ANDREW. 'Early Essex Wykehamists', *E.Rev.* 16, 1907, 173-5. List of students at New College, Oxford, 14-17th c.

CLARK, ANDREW. 'Essex and Balliol College', *E.Rev.* 21, 1912, 9-15. Brief list of Essex students to 1801, and of the rectors of Tendring, Marks Tey, and St. Leonards, Colchester.

Histories and registers of particular schools may also be useful. The list which follows is not intended to be comprehensive; rather, it aim to identify works which have particular value to genealogists, providing names of teachers and students, and other helpful information.

Belchamp St. Paul

EBELING, MARGARET. 'The village school in Belchamp St. Paul, Essex, 1887', *E.F.H.* 50, 1988, 18-19. List of pupils.

Brentwood

BEAN, E. *A historical sketch of Sir Anthony Browne's School, Brentwood, Essex, 1557-1913.* [Brentwood: The School], 1913. Lists headmasters and mentions many other names.

LEWIS, R.R. *The history of Brentwood School.* Brentwood: the Governers, 1981. Extensive; includes much information on masters and patrons.

SHANAHAN, D. 'Brentwood School and the Greenwood family', *E.Rev.* 5(1), 1963, 4-11. 16-17th c.

Chelmsford

JOHNSON, J.H. 'Chelmsford Grammar School', *E.Rev.* **54**, 1945, 45-51, 100-106 & 146-9; **55**, 1946, 1-4, 69-80, 113-7 & 180-86. Includes transcript of accounts, 1658-78, with many names.

WHEATLEY, N.J., ed. *King Edward VI School, Chelmsford commemoration book 1551-1951.* Chelmsford: J.H.Clarke & Co., [1951]. Includes extensive list of 'Old Chelmsfordians', 19-20th c.

Chigwell

STOTT, GODFREY. *A history of Chigwell School.* Ipswich: W.S.Cowell, 1960. Includes lists of boys to 1868, of governors, and of masters, *etc.*

SWALLOW, CANON. *Chigwell register, with a historical account of the school,* ed. O.W. Darch and A.S. Tween. Buckhurst Hill: J.W.Phelp, 1907. Mainly 19th c., includes lists of staff.

The Chigwell kalendar and ten year book 1887. Rivington, 1887. Includes school roll, 1877-87, list of headmasters from 1629, assistant masters from 1870, *etc.*

Colchester

ACLAND, C.L. 'Liber scholae Colcestriensis', *T.E.A.S.* N.S., **2**, 1884, 91-100 & 251-8. Discussion of a 17th c. manuscript, with names of pupils *etc.*

ROUND, J.H., ed. *Register of the scholars admitted to Colchester School 1637-1740.* Colchester: Essex Archaeological Society, 1897.

'Suffolk boys at Colchester Grammar School, 1637-1737', *E.A.M.* **1916**, 58, 60, 62-3 & 65.

Felsted

CRAZE, MICHAEL. *A history of Felstead School, 1564-1947.* Ipswich: Cowell, 1955. Includes roll of honour, etc.

SARGEAUNT, J. *A history of Felstead School, with some account of the founder and his descendants.* Chelmsford: Edmund Durrant, 1889.

WRIGHT, G.J. HORNSBY. *Alumni Felstediensis: being a list of boys entered at Felstead School from its foundation to May 1903.* Felstead: Old Felstedian Society, 1903.

MOLLER, F.S. *Alumni Felstediensis, being a list of boys entered at Felstead School, May 1564 - September 1931.* Chelmsford: Essex Weekly News, 1931.

CHITTOCK, C., ed. *Alumni Felstediensis, being a list of boys entered at Felstead School, April 1890 - September 1950.* 7th ed. Old Felstedian Society, 1951.

LOCKWOOD, E.H. *Alumni Felstediensis, January 1900 - September 1970.* 9th ed. Felstead: Old Felstedian Society, 1971.

BEEVOR, R.J. 'Felstead School', *E.Rev.* **12**, 1903, 113-5. List of boys, pre-1813.

Grays Thurrock

BROOKS, HERBERT EDMUND. *William Palmer and his school, being an account of the founder of Palmer's Charity at Grays, Essex, and his family connections; of the development of the school which bears his name; of the masters who served the school, and of the trustees who, for a century and a half, controlled the trust estate.* Colchester: Benham and Company, 1928. Includes many biographical notices.

TURNER, OLIVE. 'Two masters of Palmer's school, Grays: John and William Horncastle, 1781-1848', *Thurrock Historical Society Journal* **2**, 1957, 21-32.

Halstead

DOWNEY, MARY, & POTTS, DOREEN. *Schools and scholars in Halstead and district.* Halstead: Halstead and District Local History Society, 1986. Includes many group photographs with names.

Maldon

PETCHEY, WILLIAM JOHN. *Maldon Grammar School, 1608-1958: with an account of the earlier grammar schools of the borough, 1407-1608.* Maldon: [ ], 1958. Includes list of masters.

Newport

THOMPSON, F. *Sons of Joyce Frankland: some record of the boys of Newport Grammar School.* 2 vols. Saffron Walden: The Old Newportonian Society, 1979-84. v.1. 1588-1945. v.2. 1946-76.

Walthamstow

BOSWORTH, GEORGE F. *Essex Hall, Walthamstow and the Cogan associations.* Walthamstow Antiquarian Society, Official publication **5**. 1918. School history; includes names of pupils who presented a painting to Rev E. Cogan in 1828.

PIKE, ELSIE, CURRER, CONSTANCE E., & MOORE, U.K. *The story of Walthamstow Hall.* Otford: Longmore Press, 1973. History of a school.

POND, C.C. *George Monoux's School, Walthamstow 1527-1977.* Monograph (new series) **20**. Walthamstow Antiquarian Society, 1977. Includes list of masters.

Woodford

FRANCOMBE, D.C.R., & COULT, D.E., eds. *Bancroft's School, 1737-1937.* Woodford: Privately published, 1937. At Woodford; includes notes on Bancroft family, various lists of names, *etc*

16. MIGRATION

A. *Emigration*

Essex migrants played an important role in colonizing New England in the seventeenth century. The major study of their activities is:

THOMPSON, ROGER. *East Anglian founders of New England 1629-1640.* Amherst: University of Massachusetts Press, 1994. An investigation of the life histories of migrants from Essex, Suffolk, Norfolk, Lincolnshire, and Cambridgeshire; includes various lists of migrants.

See also:

BANKS, CHARLES EDWARD. *The Winthrop fleet of 1630: an account of the vessels, the passengers, and their English homes, from original authorities.* Boston: Houghton Mifflin, 1930. Biographical notes on passengers, who came from twenty counties, but primarily Suffolk, Essex and London.

'Essex', in COLDHAM, PETER WILSON. *Bonded passengers to America, vol. 4: home counties 1655 - 1775.* Baltimore: Genealogical Publishing, 1983, 158-207.

A number of articles also provide useful information:

CHESTER, JOSEPH LEMUEL. 'Essex families and nomenclature in New England', *T.E.A.S.* **4**, 1869, 189-96.

CHESTER, JOSEPH LEMUEL. 'The influence of the County of Essex on the settlement and family history of New England', *T.E.A.S.* **3**, 1863, 37-47.

TYACK, NORMAN C.P. 'The humbler puritans of East Anglia and the New England movement: evidence from the court records of the 1630's', *New England historical and genealogical register* **138**, 1984, 79-106.

B. *Immigration*

In the sixteenth and seventeenth centuries, Essex attracted many immigrants from the continent. Some of these were Huguenots, for which see section 12C above. See also the references listed in Raymond's *English genealogy: a bibliography.* The following may also be noted:

HARDY, W.J. 'Foreign settlers at Colchester and Halstead', *Proceedings of the Huguenot Society of London.* **2,** 1887, 182-96. Based on depositions in Court of Exchequer records, 1618; includes brief biographical notes.

ROKER, L.F. 'The Flemish and Dutch community in Colchester in the sixteenth and seventeenth centuries', *Proceedings of the Huguenot Society of London* **21**(1), 1966, 15-30. General discussion.

Author Index

A., F. 44, 45
Acland, C. 77
Adams, S. 25
Allen, D. 53
Alsford, S. 55
Andrews, H. 74
Anstruther, G. 26, 65
Appleby, D. 22
Appleby, J. 22
Arnold-Wallinger, R. 27, 30, 31
Ashton, R. 65
Astle, T. 71, 74
Austen, F. 16, 29, 30, 49, 50, 56, 62
Austen, J. 57
Austin, D. 32
Austin, F. 42
Austin, H. 34, 36

B., H. 60
B., W. 70
Baker, J. 36
Bamford, E. 41
Banbury, P. 23
Banham, D. 27
Banks, C. 78
Bannard, H. 52
Barker, R. 11, 14
Barnes, H. 30
Barnes, P. 69
Barns, S. 37, 57, 73
Barry, S. 73
Barwell, J. 74
Bates, M. 9
Batsford, M. 63
Baxter, J. 37, 54, 57
Bayley, T. 29, 38, 62
Bean, E. 76
Beaumont, G. 13, 69
Beckett, D. 24
Beckett, J. 74
Beevor, R. 77
Bell, A. 62
Benham, G. 70
Benham, H. 22, 24
Benham, M. 33

Benham, W. 19, 39, 55, 60, 73
Bennett-Bamford, A 36
Benton, A. 30
Benton, G. 23, 32, 38-42, 44, 57, 58, 62
Benton, P. 16
Benton, T. 15, 37
Bettley, J. 21
Bingley, R. 14
Birch, W. 68
Blagg, T. 27
Blaxill, E. 63
Bloom, J. 34
Bone, K. 33, 39
Bonfield, L. 10
Booker, J. 11
Bosworth, G. 57, 71, 73, 76, 78
Boutflower, C. 57
Boyden, P. 25
Brabrook, E. 42
Bradford, J. 34
Bren, R. 40
Brewer, J. 15
Bridge, H. 53
Briggs, N. 24, 32, 38, 39, 66
Britnell, R. 13, 55
Bromwich, C. 14
Brooke, C. 69
Brooker, J. 51
Brooks, C. 61
Brooks, H. 77
Broughton, T. 41
Brown, A. 11-13
Brown, E. 63
Brown, H. 12
Brown, J. 44
Brown, P. 27
Brown, R. 27, 39
Browne, A. 52
Browne, R. 27, 28, 31, 43, 59
Bryant, M. 48
Budgen, W. 68
Bullen, R. 26, 52
Bullock, L. 66

Burke, H. 30
Burley, K. 11
Burnett, M. 38
Burrows, J. 24
Butcher, C. 32

C., H. 63
C., J. 64
Cam, H. 53, 57
Campbell, J. 64
Cannadine, D. 13
Carter, H. 37
Carter, T. 24
Carus-Wilson, E. 10
Catty, M. 26
Caunt, G. 45
Chancellor, F. 16, 31-37, 60-62, 74
Charnock, R. 48
Chase, M. 23
Chester, J. 78
Chettle, H. 60
Chibnall, M. 67
Chittock, C. 77
Christy, M. 21, 32-34, 39, 40
Clark, A. 23, 28, 29, 34, 45, 50, 52, 54, 56, 61, 70, 71, 76
Clark, D. 64
Clark, R. 24
Clarke, D. 11
Clifford, H. 74
Clifford, T. 32
Clutton, G. 65
Cockburn, J. 11, 15, 53
Cockell, D. 38
Cockerill, C. 11
Cocks, H. 74
Coldewey, J. 10
Coldham, P. 78
Collins, A. 33
Collins, E. 75
Collins, T. 49
Colvin, R. 52
Commonwealth War
    Graves Commission 23
Cook, S. 54

Cooper, J 10
Cornwall, J. 50
Coult, D. 78
Coverdale, P. 30, 64
Coxall, J. 25
Cranmer-Byng, J. 24
Craze, M. 61, 77
Crisp, F. 27-30, 32
Cromarty, D. 72
Cross, A. 23
Crouch, C. 37
Crouch, W. 40
Cunningham, W. 69
Cunnington, H. 54
Currer, C. 78
Cuttle, G. 12

D'Cruze, S. 13, 22
Daniel, R. 21
Dann, G. 11
Darch, O. 77
Dare, E. 15
Davey, C. 15
Davidoff, L. 11
Davids, T. 62
Davidson, A. 44
Davies, G. 61
Davis, J. 10
Dawson, H. 63
Day, H. 22
Dean, D. 16
Deedes, C. 14, 58
Denman, H. 55
Dickin, E. 13, 59, 70
Dilliway, R. 55
Dodds, J. 63
Doolittle, I. 13
Doubleday, H. 10
Dow, L. 37
Downey, M. 77
Dunkin, A. 33
Duvall, J. 75
Dymond, D. 15

E., T. 34
East of London Family
  History Society 50, 51
Ebeling, M. 76
Eddy, M. 43
Edwards, A. 9, 10
Edwards, F. 22, 56
Eeles, H. 24
Eland, G. 71
Elliot, B. 23

Elliot, H. 37, 40
Elliott, N. 64
Ellis, H. 9
Emler, F. 62
Emmison, F. 9-11, 17, 18,
  21, 40-42, 44, 48, 53, 54,
  66, 70, 72, 73
Erith, E. 58
Erith, F. 50
Esdaile, A. 39
Essex Archaeological
  Society 18
Essex Record Office 25
Evans, B. 47, 57
Ewen, C. 25

F., K. 69
Fairweather, F. 38
Farmer, J. 21
Farries, K. 22
Feather, F. 23
Finch, P. 24
Fisher, J. 49, 67, 68, 70,
  71, 75
Fisher, W. 9
Fitch, E. 52
Fitch, M. 40, 66
Fitch, S. 63
Foley, B. 23, 64
Forby, R. 49
Forster, T. 30
Foster, S. 67
Fowler, R. 58, 59
Francombe, D. 78
Franks, A. 32
Freeth, S. 32
French, E. 44, 45
French, J. 49
Fry, G. 42
Fry, K. 14
Fryde, E. 50
Furber, E. 53

G., G. 30
Galpin, F. 34, 58, 61
Gant, L. 22
Gatfield, G. 28
Gepp, E. 28, 49, 56
Gervers, M. 68
Gibbons, T. 14, 24
Gibbs, M. 68
Gibson, E. 16, 30
Gibson, R. 12

Gilbert, W. 25, 39, 41
Girling, F. 22
Glasscock, J. 26
Glencross, R. 26
Golding, C. 27
Goodall, J. 39
Goodes, A. 27, 60
Goodwin, J. 27
Gough, A. 62
Gough, C. 21
Gough, R. 16
Graham, N. 25
Grant, E. 44
Grant, W. 18
Gray, A. 12
Gray, V. 18
Grieve, H. 13, 59
Grigson, F. 60
Grimes, H. 38
Grimes, R. 38
Grist, D. 57
Guildhall Library 25
Gyford, J. 16

H., A. 31, 73
Haines, A. 43
Haining, P. 25
Hale, W. 59, 68
Hall, C. 11
Hall, O. 42, 45
Hansom, J. 28
Hanson, S. 19, 37
Hardy, D. 12
Hardy, W. 79
Harris, T. 25
Harrison, A. 28, 70
Harrison, G. 39
Harrod, H. 55
Harrold, C. 36
Hart, C. 66, 69, 75
Hartharn, M. 45, 64, 65
Harvey, W. 38
Hassall, W. 68
Hay, E. 35
Hayston, J. 55, 56
Heaps, J. 21
Heeley d. 23
Heffer, R. 21, 75
Henderson, J. 12
Hennessy, G. 59
Henney, J. 17
Herrick, J. 63
Hewitt, G. 59
Higgs, L. 13

Historical Manuscripts
  Commission 53, 66-68
Hobson, T. 68
Hodge, E. 18
Hoff, H. 41
Hoffman, A. 60
Holcroft, W. 53
Holder, L. 22
Holdsworth, J. 52
Holman, W. 14
Holmes, C. 11
Holmes, J. 74
Holt, T. 44
Hope, T. 21, 60
Hope, W. 38, 43
Hopkins, S. 52, 57
Hopkirk, M. 55
Horwood, A. 66
Howard, E. 53
Howard, J. 30
Howell, E. 18
Howell, T. 72
Howlett, G. 55
Huelin, G. 64
Hughes, L. 15
Hull, F. 48, 71
Humphery-Smith, C. 26
Humphreys, D. 57
Hunt, E. 23
Hunt, W. 11
Hunter, R. 56
Hutchings, A. 55
Hutchinson, D. 63

Imperial War Graves
  Commission 23

Jarvis, C. 12
Jarvis, L. 16
Jarvis, S. 9
Jeaffreson, J. 53, 67
Jeayes, I. 55, 70, 73
Jeffers, R. 75
Johnson, G. 29
Johnson, J. 77
Johnston, G. 29
Jones, I. 66
Judson, E. 25

K. 31
Kelway, A. 32
Kennedy, J. 15
Kent, A. 39
Kentish, B. 15

Kenworthy, J. 60
King, H. 19, 27, 38, 41, 44,
  45, 59, 74, 75
Kingston, A. 11
Kirk, R. 66
Knell, P. 64, 65

L., F. 40
L'Estrange, J. 19
Langton, F. 28
Lart, C. 30
Laver, H. 19
Law, A. 37, 62
Le May, D. 54
Lea, J. 43
Levine, D. 16
Lewer, H. 43
Lewis, R. 38, 77
Lexden, H. 35
Liddell, W. 10
Litten, J. 37
Loades, D. 59
Lockwood, E. 77
Lockwood, H. 12, 18, 29
Loftus, E. 60
Lowndes, G. 42, 74
Lyndon, B. 11
Lysons, D. 9
Lyte, H. 68

Macaulay, J. 72
Macfarlane, A. 11, 14, 25
Majende, L. 55
Malden, H. 41
Manning, C. 38
Markham, C. 35
Marshall, G. 26, 38
Martin, G. 9, 13, 54
Mary Catherine, Sister
  33-37, 64
Mason, A. 22
Mason, B. 21
Mason, E. 25
Matthews, R. 46
Mcintosh, M. 14, 52, 61, 71
Mclachlan, M. 50
Mcmaster, I. 76
Moens, W. 28
Moller, F. 77
Moon, Z. 17
Moore, S. 67
Moore, U. 78
Morant, P. 13, 30
Moss, L. 45

Moss, R. 45
Murrells, D. 48
Muskett, J. 43

N., J. 67, 70
Neale, K. 9, 41, 50
Newcourt, R. 59
Newman, H. 21
Newnham, L. 21
Newton, K. 18, 19, 53, 72,
  73
Nicholas, Mother 64
Nichols, J. 70-72
Nolan, M. 45, 60, 64
Nolan, N. 26
Norden, J. 9
Norris, E. 43
Norris, L. 37
Norris, M. 37
Nurse, B. 15
Nutt, J. 26

O'Connor, S. 67
O'Dwyer, M. 64
O'Leary, J. 13, 38, 42, 48,
  64, 72
Ogborne, E. 9
Oman, C. 50
Orridge, B. 10
Osborne, D. 28
Owen, J. 65
Oxley, J. 10, 54, 67, 69

P., A. 16
P., M. 73
P., R. 39
Page, W. 10
Pagenstecher, G. 14
Palin, W. 16
Palmer, C. 60
Park, S. 29, 35
Parker, R. 24
Partridge, C. 31, 37, 72
Patchett, A. 14
Petchey, W. 15, 77
Phillimore, W. 27-29, 31
Phillips, A. 55, 63
Piggot, J. 38
Pike, E. 78
Pleydell, P. 23
Pohl, D. 15
Pond, C. 78
Poole, R. 68
Poos, L. 10
Porteous, W. 32-34, 39, 40

Potts, D. 77
Powell, J. 38
Powell, W 10
Powell, W. 10, 17, 73
Pressey, W. 55, 56, 58-60
Preston, H. 21
Probert, C. 31
Probert, G. 38
Probert, W. 31

Quaife, J. 70
Quintrell, B. 52

R., G. 58
Rackham, O. 14
Radcliffe, W. 22
Ramsey, A. 22
Ransford, A. 44
Ratcliffe, R. 26
Rayment, J. 26
Razi, Z. 69
Reaney, P. 43, 48, 60, 62,
  66, 69, 72, 73
Redman, M. 34
Reid, E. 61
Rendall, G. 38, 55
Rickword, G. 19, 22, 44,
  49, 52, 55, 61, 70, 71
Ritchie, N. 10
Robin, J. 14
Roe, E. 70
Roebuck, C. 30
Roebuck, G. 28-30
Roker, L. 79
Round, J. 10, 17, 43, 73-77
Rowley, N. 53, 76
Rowntree, C. 28, 72
Rumble, A. 49
Rush, J. 73
Russell, I. 72
Ryan, P. 43
Rye, W. 49

S. 43, 56
Sage, E. 42, 43
Sainsbury, F. 17, 57
Salzman, L. 68
Samaha, J. 11
Sargeaunt, J. 77
Scargill-Bird, S. 71
Schofield, P. 69
Scollan, M. 22
Scott, W. 74
Searle, A. 42
Sellers, E. 43

Shanahan, D. 26, 77
Sharpe, J. 11, 15, 53
Sharpe, P. 11, 12
Shawcross, J. 13
Sier, L. 21, 39, 70, 71, 74,
  75
Simpson, W. 69
Skeet, F. 45
Slade, C. 69
Smith, B. 32, 61
Smith, C. 19, 22, 30
Smith, E. 32, 33
Smith, H. 14, 26, 28, 29,
  52, 57, 59, 60, 62
Smith, J. 11, 60
Smith, R. 10, 16, 69
Sokoll, T. 12
Somerset, H. 44
Sparkes, I. 18
Sparvel-Bayly, J. 71
Spaul, J. 43
Spence, J. 16
Sperling, C. 28, 53, 61, 74
Sreenivasan, G. 14
Stacey, H. 57, 63, 72
Stahlschmidt, J. 43, 45
Stedman, A. 66
Steer, F. 31, 40, 42, 44, 48,
  57, 68
Steinman, G. 36, 67
Stephens, R. 11
Stephenson, P. 28
Stott, G. 77
Strathern, M. 14
Strutt, B. 13
Stuart, N. 31
Stuchfield, H. 35
Studd, P. 16
Sturt, N. 27-29
Styles, J. 15
Suckling, A. 9
Summers, P. 32
Swallow, Canon 77
Sworder, C. 56
Symonds, G. 62

Tabor, M. 15
Tancock, O. 25, 27
Tempie, F. 75
Thompson, F. 78
Thompson, R. 78
Thompson, T. 22
Tinworth, W. 15
Titterton, J. 32

Tonkin, W. 37
Tooley, R. 48
Trinder, J. 23
Turner, O. 76, 77
Tween, A. 77
Tyack, N. 78

Usher, R. 59

Vaughan, E. 75

Wadley, T. 44
Wakeling, A. 23
Walcott, E. 60
Walker, K. 19, 74
Wall, R. 12
Waller, W. 15, 21, 30, 42,
  57, 59, 63, 69, 70, 72, 73
Walter, J. 15
Walters, H. 58
Ward, B. 22
Ward, C. 12, 27
Ward, G. 17
Ward, J. 10, 13, 49
Watson, J. 16
Watson, P. 22
Webb, C. 17, 31
Wells, E. 58
West, A. 61
Westlake, H. 68
Wheatley, N. 77
White, W. 46
Whitley, W. 63
Whitmore, F. 24
Whitwood, C. 57
Wilcox, A. 25
Williams, J. 40, 43, 56, 72
Wilson, T. 42
Winstone, B. 56
Winters, W. 30, 62, 72
Wolfston, P. 31
Wood, A. 16
Wood, R. 10, 11
Woodgate, J. 22
Woodward, D. 11
Worley, G. 58
Worral, E. 65
Worrall, E. 27, 29, 30, 34,
  64, 65
Worrall, J. 64
Wright, C. 63
Wright, D. 11
Wright, G. 77
Wright, T. 9
Wrightson, K. 10, 16

Family Name Index

Adly 42
Appleton 64
Atslow 64

Bacon 10
Baker 56, 75
Baldock 59
Bancroft 78
Barfoot 37
Barnes 37
Barrington 66
Barsley 76
Barton 64
Beaucock 37
Berdefeld 74
Bigesby 76
Blyth 42
Borrell 37
Boteler 38
Bourchier 38, 44, 74, 75
Bourne 32
Brand 14
Braybrooke 38, 67
Bridge 34
Browne 38
Buckingham 74
Burford 45

Cade 10
Cammocke 38
Capell 67
Chisenhale-Marsh 72
Church 64
Cleveland 43
Cocke 75
Cogan 78
Coggeshall 13
Coleman 34
Collard 76
Convers 43
Cooke 10, 43
Cooper 67
Cornwallis 67
Cosens 63
Cox 34
Crowley 45
Crush 43
Curgenven 39

Cutts 74

Darcy 38, 64
Davyson 70
De Barr 72
De Vere 38, 43
Deane 34
Dikes 13
Dunstanville 39

Eastry 38
Edwards 43
Ennows 43

Fanshawe 43
Fitzherbert 37
Fitzralph 38
Flamberds 38
Forder 76
Fortescue 74
Frankland 78
Fraunceys 67

Gamgee 14
Garnon 57
Gayselee 38
Gedge 74
Gerard 43
Gernin 57
Gernon 38
Gestingthorpe 14
Gibson 22
Giffard 38
Gosnold 43
Gravesend 59
Greenhill 14
Greenwood 77
Gwynne 75

Hammond 14
Harlakenden 67
Harris 74
Harsnett 43
Harwich 14
Hayes 14
Haynes 43
Heird 43
Hervey 43

Honywood 39
Horncastle 77
Houblon 74
Houghton 44
Hoy 14
Hurrel 76

Jennings 64
Josselyn 44

Kendale 39
King 19

Larder 39
Lathum 16
Laxham 37
Lean 39
Leapingwell 15
Lince 13
Lovell 44
Lowndes 66, 73

Malb 44
Marler 15
Marney 44, 71
Martin 75
Maxey 67
Maynard 52
Merell 44
Monteny 44
Montgomery 74
Mordaunt 39
More 44
Morfee 13
Morley 44, 74
Morse 44

Newport 59
Nicholls 44
Nugent 74
Nutman 76

Oliver 32

Palmer 77
Parker 39
Partridge 39, 72
Pelly 76
Petre 23, 37, 39, 44, 67

Phillipson 34
Pinchon 37
Piryton 44
Playter 44
Pyel 67

Rainsford 44
Rebow 44
Reeves 14
Rhodes 39
Rich 39, 75
Riche 33, 44
Rochester 39
Rogers 38
Ryves 45

Savage 64
Segrave 59
Sewell 45

Sinclair 33
Smith 30, 39
Smythies 13
Soones 45
Sorrell 45
St Clere 33
Stanley 40
Stephenson 45
Strype 40
Sudburia 59
Sysley 45

Tanfield 40
Tedcastell 40
Tey 75
Thoroughgood 65
Toller 43
Turnor 74

Urswick 75

Waldegrave 40, 45, 64
Wanton 45
Warner 45
Waylett 64
Wellesley 45
Weston 37
Whitbred 45, 64
Whitmore 75
Whittingham 76
Wilford 45
Wingfield 75
Winterfludd 64
Winthrop 78
Wiseman 45, 64, 74
Woodthorpe 40
Wright 44

Young 22

Place Name Index

Bedfordshire 46
Arlesey 72

Berkshire 19

Buckinghamshire 19

Cambridgeshire 9, 11, 19, 24, 26, 46, 60, 64, 72

Cornwall
Lelant 39

Devon 68
Colyton 16
Plymouth 30
Stonehouse 30

Dorset 68

Essex 10, 19, 32, 34, 40, 43
Adulvesnasa 68
Ardleigh 50
Ardley 43
Arkesden 31, 32
Ashdon 12, 27, 49
Ashen 69
Audley End 67
Aveley 16, 18, 32, 47, 54, 60
Bacons 71, 74
Barking 12, 17, 18, 27, 32, 40, 42, 50, 54, 63, 69, 74
Barking Abbey 60, 67, 69
Barling 68
Barnston 27, 50
Barrington Hall 66, 73
Barringtons Fee 69
Beaumont 27
Becontree Hundred 9, 10, 53, 65
Beeleigh Abbey 44
Belchamp Saint Paul 68, 76
Benfleet 19, 46, 54, 69
Billericay 46
Birch 32
Birchanger 68
Birdbrooke 69
Blackmore 12
Bobbingworth 27, 32

Bocking 21, 27, 46, 60
Bocking Deanery 60
Boreham 27, 33, 50
Boreham. New Hall 65, 73
Borley 33, 40, 44, 69
Bowers Gifford 33
Boxted 27
Bradwell Juxta Mare 12
Braintree 46, 50, 54, 60
Braybrooke 67
Brentwood 39, 46, 77
Brightlingsea 13, 23, 70
Buckhurst Hill 48
Bulmer 33
Bulmers 65
Bulphan 16, 18, 54
Bures 38
Burnham 54, 55, 70
Buttsbury 64
Canewdon 54
Canvey Island 46
Chadwell Saint Mary 16, 18, 47, 55
Chafford Hundred 10
Chatham Hall 70
Chelmsford 13, 21, 27, 46, 50, 55, 60, 63, 64, 70, 77
Chelmsford. Guy Harlings 74
Chignal 60
Chigwell 21, 23, 42, 48, 70, 77
Childerditch 50
Chingford 19, 27, 33, 40, 48, 55, 68
Chingford Hall 73
Clacton 47
Coggeshall 13, 44, 45, 63
Colchester 10, 11, 13, 19, 21-23, 27, 33, 43, 44, 47, 49, 50, 52, 55, 60, 61, 63, 65, 70, 77, 79
Colchester. Greenstead Manor 71
Colchester. Helen's Lane 63
Colchester. Saint Johns Abbey 67
Colchester Castle 73
Colchester Deanery 61
Colchester Union 55
Colne Engaine 74
Colne Priory 68
Copford Hall 70
Corringham 16, 18
Cranham 50

Essex (*continued*)
Crondon Park 28
Dagenham 13, 17, 18, 48, 50, 75
Danbury 28, 42, 55, 61
Debden 28
Dedham 38, 44, 55, 59, 61
Dengie 50
Dovercourt 34, 47
Downham 33
Dunmow 47, 55
Dunton 18
Earls Colne 14, 44, 70
Earls Fee 70
East Hall 70
East Ham 47, 55
East India Docks 22
East Mersea 70
East Tilbury 16
Eastbury Hall 45
Easthorpe 28
Easton Lodge 69
Epping 21, 40, 47, 51, 56, 63
Epping Forest 56
Epping Place 74
Fairstead 33
Faulkbourne 33, 74
Felsted 33, 39, 49, 56, 61, 67, 70, 77
Felsted. Bannister Green 28
Finchingfield 34, 35, 54, 56
Fingringhoe 42, 70, 73
Fobbing 14, 16, 18
Forest Gate 48
Foulness 70
Foxearth 44
Frating 34
Fryerning 19, 32, 61
Fyfield 28
Gaines 70
Gaynes Park 72
Gidea Hall 10
Gobions 70
Goodmayes 47
Gosfield Hall 74
Grays 26, 47, 56, 77
Grays Thurrock 16, 56
Great Baddow 45
Great Bromley 42
Great Canfield 71
Great Dunmow 56, 61, 71, 74
Great Hallingbury 56
Great Henny 34, 71, 75
Great Ilford 50
Great Leighs 32, 54, 61
Great Leighs. Lyons Hall 71

Great Maplestead 61, 74
Great Oakley 67
Great Tey 61, 71
Great Waltham 39, 70
Great Warley 50
Greenstead 28
Hadleigh 46, 54
Hadleigh Castle 71
Hallingbury 74
Halstead 28, 38, 44, 45, 77, 79
Harlow 34, 56, 71
Harlow Hundred 10
Harwich 14, 34, 47, 51, 52, 56
Hatfield Broad Oak 61, 66, 74
Hatfield Peverel 50
Hatfield Priory 66
Havering 14, 17, 50, 52, 71
Havering, Liberty of 9, 10
Hempstead 38, 39
Heybridge 56
Heydon 44
High Beach 47
High Easter 56, 61
Highwood 34
Hinckford Hundred 50
Hockney 46
Holland on Sea 47
Horham 45, 74
Hornchurch 45, 50, 68
Hornchurch Priory 61
Horndon 15, 16, 45
Hutton 35, 45, 71
Ilford 29, 47
Ingatestone 19, 23, 35, 39, 65, 67
Ingatestone. Brook Cottage 74
Ingrave 35, 38
Jay Wick 47, 74
Kelvedon 15, 35, 70
Kelvedon Hall 44
Kelvedon Hatch. Great Myles 74
Kelvedon. Church Hall Manor 70
Killegrews 74
Laindon 16
Lambourne 29, 37
Langham 42
Langham. Valley House 74
Lawford Hall 75
Lawling 71
Layer de la Haye 75
Layer Marney 71
Leigh on Sea 48
Leyton 15, 35, 40, 48, 51
Leytonstone 15, 47, 48
Leytonstone. Wallwood 75

Lindsell 32, 68
Little Baddow 35
Little Birch 61
Little Braxted 35
Little Clacton 47
Little Dunmow 38
Little Horkesley 44
Little Ilford 47
Little Leighs 61
Little Oakley 67
Little Parndon 56
Little Stambridge 75
Little Thurrock 15, 16, 47
Little Wakering 54
Little Waltham 45, 61
Loughton 15, 23, 40, 47, 48
Maldon 15, 38, 51, 52, 56, 77
Malgraves 37
Manor Park 47
Margaretting 40, 64
Marks 75
Mersea 15
Milton Hall 71, 72
Moreton 15, 29
Mountnessing 44
Moze 29, 67
Mucking 16, 18
Navestock 33, 35, 68
Nazeing 40, 62, 72
Netteswellbury 75
Newham 17-19, 29, 35, 51
Newport 15, 78
North Benfleet 46
Norton 68
Ongar 29, 47
Ongar Hundred 9, 10, 72
Orsett 15, 16, 18, 35, 47, 64, 75
Pebmarsh 29, 38, 62, 75
Peldon 62
Pentlow 35
Pete Hall 70
Plaistow 48
Pleshey 16
Prittlewell 29, 54, 70
Purfleet 18, 47
Quendon 45
Rainham 36, 50, 74
Ramsden Bellhouse 50, 56, 62
Ramsden Crays 64, 72
Ramsden Heath 50
Ramsey Abbey 68
Ramsey. Roydon Hall 75
Rayne. Netherhouse 75
Rayne. Turners 75

Redbridge 17, 18, 26
Rettendon 36
Rivenhall 36
Rochford 19, 54
Rochford Hundred 57
Romford 19, 36, 43, 47, 50, 52, 57
Romford. Marshalls 75
Roxwell 30, 42, 43
Rukholde 69
Runwell 36, 62, 68
Saffron Walden 47, 51, 57, 62, 72
Saffron Walden. High Street 72, 75
Saint Osyth 47
Saint Osyth's Priory 68
Salcott 62
Seven Kings 47
Shalford 32, 43
Shapland 34
Shelley 75
Skighaw 67
Snaresbrook 47, 48
Soken 44
South Benfleet 54
South Ockendon 62
South Weald 36
Southend 48
Springfield 36
Stambourne 32, 72
Stanford le Hope 16, 47
Stanford Rivers 57
Stanway 16, 36
Stebbing 34
Steeple Grange 72
Stifford 16, 18, 32, 47
Stisted 30
Stock 16, 30, 42, 50, 62, 64
Stondon Massey 16
Stratford 30, 48
Stratford Langthorne Abbey 69
Sutton 54
Takeley 68
Tendring 51
Tendring Hundred 73
Terling 16, 36, 39, 57
Thaxted 62
Theydon Bois 47
Theydon Garnon 36, 57, 62, 72
Theydon Mount 75
Thorndon 35, 65
Thorpe Le Soken 16, 63
Thorrington 72, 75
Thundersley 54
Thurrock 19, 21, 30, 36
Tidwoldington 68

Tilbury 18, 47
Tillingham 37, 68
Tilty Abbey 69
Toppesfield 30
Upminster 37, 42, 50, 63, 70
Vange 46
Waltham Abbey. Sun Street 75
Waltham Holy Cross 30, 40, 62, 72
Waltham Hundred 9, 10
Walthamstow 16, 19, 23, 25, 30, 37, 40,
    42, 48, 51, 57, 62, 63, 71, 76, 78
Walthamstow. High Hall 73
Walthamstow. Low Hall 71
Walthamstow. Salisbury Hall 71, 72
Walthamstow Toni 73
Wanstead 20, 47, 48, 50, 51, 57
Weeks 67
Wendens Ambo 62
Wennington 36, 50
West Bergholt. Garlands 76
West Ham 48, 57
West Horndon 76
West Mersea 70, 73
West Thurrock 47, 56
West Thurrock. Bunting's Farm 76
West Tilbury 16
Westcliff 48
Wethersfield 44, 73
Wickford 46
Wickham Bishops 37
Wickham Saint Paul 68
Widdington 68
Willingale Doe 12
Willingale Spain 12
Wimbish 45
Witham 16, 31, 35, 51
Witham Place 65
Wivenhoe 57, 58, 73
Wix Priory 69
Woodford 19, 31, 37, 40, 48, 52, 58, 62
Woodgrange 34
Woodham Ferrers 73
Wormingford 31
Writtle 31, 34, 37, 40, 45, 68, 73
Wykes 73

Essex, South 54

Essex, West 48

Gloucestershire 67
Bristol 30

Hampshire 67
Portsmouth 21

Hertfordshire 9, 11, 19, 40, 43, 44, 46,
    67-69
Watford. Cassiobury Park 67

Huntingdonshire 11, 46

Kent 10, 46, 48
Dungeness 22

Lancashire
Hopcar 28
Pendleton 21

Leicestershire
Bottesford 16
Shepshed 16

Lincolnshire 11

London & Middlesex 10, 19, 28, 30, 41,
    43, 45, 46, 64, 67, 68, 78
Clerkenwell. Saint Mary's Nunnery 68
Hackney 43
Hammersmith 65
Saint Botolph, Bishopsgate 26
Saint Pauls Cathedral 69
Stepney 26

Norfolk 9, 11, 19, 22, 26, 44, 46, 60, 64,
    66, 67

Northamptonshire 67
Northampton 72

Oxfordshire 44
Oxford. New College 68

Suffolk 9, 11, 12, 19, 22, 24, 28, 46, 60, 64,
    66, 78
Bury Saint Edmunds 71

Suffolk, South 48

Surrey 19, 46, 68
Richmond 73

Sussex 46
Battle Abbey 71
Lewes 68
Lewes Priory 68

Sussex, East 48

Warwickshire
Birmingham 11

Wiltshire 68

Yorkshire
Whitby 14
York 43

OVERSEAS

Belgium
Liege 65

France
Caen Abbey 67
Gravelines 34

Italy
Rome 65

United States
Rhode Island 13